Identifying People
in the Past

Identifying People in the Past

Edited by

E. A. Wrigley

EDWARD ARNOLD

© Edward Arnold (Publishers) Ltd, 1973

First published 1973
by Edward Arnold (Publishers) Ltd.,
25 Hill Street, London W1X 8LL

ISBN: 0 7131 5694 5

Printed in Great Britain by
Richard Clay (The Chaucer Press), Ltd., Bungay, Suffolk

Contents

Contributors

Yves Blayo

Chargé de recherches, Institut National d' Etudes Démographiques, Paris

David Herlihy

Professor of History, Harvard University

Roger Schofield

Director of Cambridge Group for the History of Population and Social Structure, and Fellow of Clare College, Cambridge

Mark Skolnick

Departments of Genetics at the University of Pavia and Stanford University

Ian Winchester

Assistant Professor of Philosophy in the Department of History and Philosophy, Ontario Institute for Studies in Education

Tony Wrigley

Member of Cambridge Group for the History of Population and Social Structure, and Fellow and Bursar of Peterhouse, Cambridge

E. A. Wrigley

Introduction

The essays which comprise this book are all about nominal record linkage. This is the rather clumsy expression used to denote the process by which items of information about a particular named individual are associated with each other into a coherent whole in accordance with certain rules. In recent years there has been a spate of historical studies involving nominal record linkage on a scale which requires the linkage rules to be set out formally and in detail. Most of these studies have been based on parish registers (or a comparable source of genealogical information), or on nineteenth-century census schedules.[1] And at the same time there has been a marked tendency to abandon manual methods in favour of computers. The six chapters which follow represent an attempt to describe some of the methods currently in use, and to discuss the problems and opportunities of record linkage work. Some of the jargon used will be unfamiliar to most historians,[2] but one may hope that record linkage techniques will receive sympathetic attention nonetheless, since they can be used to take us closer to the grassroots of history, bringing to light for ordinary men and women something of the detail previously known only for the literate and well-born.

The twentieth century is sometimes called the century of the common man. Many will doubt the truth of the aphorism. But it may be that it will prove to be the century in which the history of the common man, not seen through the eyes of his betters but drawn out from the workaday records of the past, became a major part of historical work. And in this regard nominal record linkage, for all its technical

[1] There are, for example, family reconstitution studies either published or in train in France (where they may be numbered by the score), Belgium, Canada, England, Estonia, Germany, Hungary, Italy, Japan, the Philippines, Poland, Scandinavia, South America and the United States. Studies based on census schedules are equally widespread.

[2] For this reason a short glossary will be found at the end of this book.

trappings, is a means of discovering things about the lives of ordinary men which would otherwise remain obscure.

It was in recognition of the promise of record linkage techniques that in May 1970 the Mathematical Social Sciences Board sponsored a conference on Nominal Record Linkage in History which was held at the Institute for Advanced Study in Princeton. This book has grown out of that meeting. Most of those who came to the conference were historians or historical demographers, but since an interest in record linkage is now widely shared, there were also sociologists and geneticists present, and a number of scholars whose interests lie partly in other fields, such as medicine, philosophy, political science and data processing. For record linkage is an operation which under-pins the assembly of information and growth of knowledge in many contexts, and it is widely practised informally even by those to whom the term itself may be unfamiliar. Indeed, many of those who have recently found points of importance to them in discussions of record linkage, have come to it much in the fashion of the man who found to his surprise that he had been talking prose all his life without realising it.

In historical work the problem turns essentially on knowing when a record about *this* William Whiston refers to the same man as *that* William Whiston (or that William, or that Whiston) mentioned in another record. In many cases, and especially where the individuals concerned were rich, or powerful, or of high status, ambiguities may be very few and such as can be dealt with by that quality of judge-ment which comes from long study of a particular man, or parlia-ment, or lineage. But there are also circumstances in which it is more convenient and more accurate to make and break links in accordance with formal rules, and without benefit of intuitive judgement. This makes for consistency and helps to avoid unconscious bias, though these attributes are often purchased only at the cost of some loss of flexibility and sensitivity to the local context. The formal rules may be used when linking records by hand, and indeed one of the most influential of all such formal systems was designed for implementa-tion by hand.[3] But they may also be expressed as a computer program and then applied to data which have been converted into machine-readable form. Given the capacity of modern electronic computers, this possibility can be alluring where there are large bodies of data to be treated.

[3] The logic of family reconstitution from vital registers was first fully worked out about twenty years ago by Louis Henry in collaboration with Michel Fleury. M. Fleury and L. Henry, *Des registres paroissiaux à l'histoire de la population: Manuel de dépouillement et d'exploitation de l'état civil ancien* (Paris, 1956).

It is easy to grow fascinated by the minutiae of record linkage, the endless series of logical and practical puzzles which arise with each new body of data. Parts of this book reflect this fascination. But record linkage is only a means to an end in most connections. It has grown more prominent in certain branches of historical study partly because of a shift in interest towards populations as a whole rather than elite groups within them, and partly because with a computer it is possible to sort, compare and link records on a much greater scale than would be feasible by hand without immense labour. It is now possible to maintain the full text of records on tape or disc and so to avoid coding out much of the information they contain on input, thus overcoming one of the weightiest objections to their use.

THE NATURE OF RECORD LINKAGE STUDIES

From linked individual records it is always possible, by aggregation, to examine the characteristics of any larger group, whereas the reverse is not true. Even though the characteristics of the group can be sketched from the tabulation of unlinked aggregate data, the behaviour of individuals may remain obscure, and the types of explanation which can be considered will be limited as a result. For example, suppose that it can be shown from aggregate statistics that there is a negative correlation between fluctuations in the price of wheat and the number of marriages in a community. The fact may be clear. How should it be interpreted?

One hypothesis might be that when wheat, and therefore bread, is cheap, real incomes are increased, especially for the majority of the population who spend a large part of their income on basic foods. This encourages couples who had previously held back from marriage because of hard times to set a date for their wedding. But in the community there will also be groups who might be expected, by the same argument, to be untouched by an influence of this type, or alternatively to display a positive rather than a negative relationship between wheat prices and marriage frequencies. Into the first class should fall those whose incomes are so high that fluctuations in the price of bread grain will not significantly affect them, while in the second might be found landholders or farmers whose incomes are highest when wheat is scarce and costly because they produce on a scale sufficient to ensure that the bulk of their production is sold off the farm. Such men benefit from times of dearth because income elasticity of demand for bread grain is low and the rise in price per unit sold in times of scarcity more than offsets the fall in the volume sold. Inasmuch as current income affects marriage among substantial farmers, therefore, it might be expected to encourage marriage when wheat prices were high.

To test the implications of an hypothesis like this entails splitting the population as a whole into smaller groups and examining their marriage patterns. For this record linkage is normally necessary. The relationship between wheat prices and marriage frequencies demonstrable in aggregate is, of course, consonant with other explanations, and may prove to be irreconcilable with the suggested hypothesis. For example, record linkage work might reveal no significant differences in marriage patterns between groups with very different economic circumstances. If so, the initial hypothesis will need to be reformulated. Equally, the hypothesis may be correct but the pattern may fail to be visible in the aggregate data because, say, the labouring poor who conform to the hypothesis in their behaviour and others who do not, are roughly equal in number. As a result the opposing influences on marriage frequencies may cancel one another out. Or again, the effect, though present, may turn out on detailed examination to be muffled by the effect of birth rank. In an area of primogeniture it is conceivable that the timing of the marriages of eldest sons might be largely unaffected by economic circumstances (since this will be controlled chiefly by the death of fathers) whereas younger sons, dependent on wage income and without the prospect of any large inheritance, might be influenced strongly by current real wage levels and employment prospects.

Nominal record linkage, in furthering the understanding of situations such as this, can perform for the past what elaborate cross-tabulation achieves today. It would be possible to cross-classify men at marriage according to their rank of birth among surviving male siblings, and then to compare eldest sons with others of different rank who were otherwise similarly placed. But descriptive statistics are rarely so elaborate even today, and tend to be inflexible even when elaborate. They cannot therefore be recast easily to bear on a particular hypothesis. Moreover, when descriptive statistics contain detailed cross-tabulations they usually cover very large areas, commonly the nation state, which may itself contain so many contrasting regions and smaller areas that relationships tend to be blurred as a result.

In short, record linkage involves high costs and, if carried out by hand, great tedium, but it can offer high rewards, too, made possible by the precision with which the test can be tailored in order to fit the hypothesis to be tested. History is always imprisoned by the range and nature of the sources of information about any given time and place. But, though the sources may prove hard to augment, techniques for using them to best advantage can from time to time be improved. Record linkage, because of its ability to articulate and structure data, gives greater depth and fuller dimension to pictures of the past that would otherwise be flat and lack perspective. Meaning is latent in sets of linked records.

IDENTIFYING INDIVIDUALS

Nominal records are those in which individuals are distinguished by name, and by that token are potentially linkable to other nominal records. There is point in doing this only when two conditions are met. First, that it can be shown that it is possible to distinguish satisfactorily between true and false links. Second, that the complex of information which can be assembled by linking records that concern one man reveals something about him which would otherwise remain obscure.

The two issues are closely connected with each other in a manner which adds piquancy to many of the arguments about record linkage. It will be obvious that the larger the number of information fields common to a pair of records, the greater will be the certainty with which a decision can be made about whether or not they should be linked, *ceteris paribus*. For example, suppose that there are two marriage records each concerning William Whiston, and the question arises whether the bridegroom in the two records was the same man or two different men. If in each record the information is sparse, consisting only of a date and the names of the bride and groom, there may be doubt as to whether or not the two records should be linked. If, on the other hand, not only is William Whiston named in both records, but his age, his place of birth, his occupation, the names of his parents and the names of any previous wives are also given, the margin of doubt will be whittled away to the vanishing point (assuming there is agreement in each information field). But the increased certainty will be offset by diminished utility, for the information in the earlier record is largely encapsulated in the later record (apart perhaps from the exact dates of the earlier event). In a limiting case there would be little point in undertaking record linkage if each record produced in the course of a man's life rehearsed all that had been embodied in earlier records. It would then be possible simply to take the last record in a series and abstract information from it. Checks upon accuracy might still be needed. Similarly, record linkage might be necessary to establish which was the last in a series of records concerning one man: but the last record would always contain all or almost all that could be gleaned from earlier records.

Contrast this with the problems and opportunities where each record contains relatively little information. Here the potential gain of information from linking records may be relatively far greater but the problems of linkage increase *pari passu*. A burial record which recorded a man's age, his occupation, his past marriages and his various children living and dead would, if accurate, leave little to be learned from discovering records of his birth, marriages and children's births. A burial record which merely stated his name would leave much to be learned from successful linkage to earlier records relating to his past life, even assuming that they too were parsimoniously phrased. The isolated record is then almost valueless if the aim is to reconstruct the life history of an individual, whereas a set of linked records each containing relatively little information may jointly provide as much information as a set of fuller records between which there is considerable overlap of information. But if the gain of information is greater in the first case, the difficulties of accurate linkage will also be greater and may easily be such as to make the exercise pointless since the links may be too fragile to be trusted.

The ideal situation is one in which one information field in each record is reserved for a unique identifier, while other information in the record is to be found only in that record and not in others. In this way as more and more records pertaining to one man are linked there is a rapid increase in information about him and what might be termed the marginal return to each additional link made is at a maximum. The less completely these two desiderata obtain the less dependable the links (where the records lack unique identifiers) or the less rapid the increase in information (where there is overlap of information between records). But though one might wish for both conditions to be met, in practice neither occurs. And there tends therefore to be a trade-off between the two so that congruity of information in several information fields is welcomed because of the added strength this gives the link between the records, even though the sum of knowledge about the individual in question is increased very little where one record largely repeats what is given in another linked to it.

NAMES AND NAME SPELLING

In modern societies there are several ways in which an attempt is made to give unique identifiers to everyone in a population. These can then be used to make record linkage certain. Fingerprints and photographs are used for this purpose by police forces. National insurance or social security numbers may be used by government bureaucracy more generally. In the past names served the same purpose—as indeed much of the time they still do today. It is reasonable to suppose that the universal adoption of surnames to supplement forenames in medieval England was due in part to their usefulness in making it easier to identify men and women more completely. Perhaps it is indirect evidence of the degree of mobility in a society when John becomes John Smith and William becomes William Harrison.[4] At all events names are usually the means by which links between historical records are initially made. Disagreement between names in two records is normally a bar to linkage, while agreement creates a *prima facie* case for linkage. Indeed if names had always been fully and consistently recorded and no two persons had ever shared the same names, it would always be clear whether or not two records should be linked. The string of letters making up a man's name would be as complete a means of identifying him as the sequence of digits which identify a particular telephone receiver. Attention could be concentrated largely upon the other information fields in a set of linked records which together define what can be known of the man's characteristics.

But names were never unique identifiers. Nor would it have helped greatly if each child at baptism had received names which no other shared. Names were so frequently abbreviated, modified, changed or dropped, and their spelling when they were written out was so often wayward, that there is a prior problem of great complexity to be solved in standardizing names before the stage of linkage proper is reached. For clearly if the most important criterion used in linking

---

[4] As an illustration of the value of adding a surname to a forename in assisting identification, consider the first hundred years of the parish registers of Colyton (1538–1640). In this period the registers contain 12,004 male forenames. The most frequently used forename by far was John (3,483 occurrences, or 29 per cent of the total), followed by William (1,434), Thomas (997) and Robert (983). During the same period the registers contain 17,393 surnames, but the most frequent surname, Newton, occurred only 324 times (less than 2 per cent of the total). There were 123 references to John Newton in the registers, larger than the expected number assuming forenames and surnames to be randomly associated, but still few enough to make identification of individuals bearing this, the commonest forename/surname combination, a vastly simpler matter than by forename alone.

records is the name in the record, it is essential to decide what shall be regarded as a variant form of a given name and what as a different name. This may not be difficult in the case of, say, Smith and Smythe, but it grows problematic when the file of records contains, say, Bull, Ball, Bawl, Baul, Bool, Boal, etc. In practice in a record file of substantial size, such as a parish register, and especially in the sixteenth and seventeenth centuries, there may be dozens of variants of what is clearly the same name, together with many more name spellings where the case is less clear cut. The matter is so important that many discussions of nominal record linkage consist very largely in the attempt to provide a method of standardizing names which will keep all character strings which are variants of the 'same' name together without at the same time including any character string which is a variant of some other name. If the method can be reduced to a simple set of operational rules for name standardization so much the better, since this will make it possible to punch the names as they are found and rely upon a suitable computer program to convert them to their standardized form.

Where most records contain several names, as in the parish register of Grisy-Suisnes of which Blayo writes later in this volume, the problem of standardizing names is the predominant issue in nominal record linkage. In addition to the names of the principal of the record, his or her parents and often other relatives are mentioned. In effect this produces much the same situation as if each individual had six or seven names himself as far as identification is concerned. It is then extremely rare for there to be more than one link which can be made from, say, a bride's marriage record to a preceding baptism. Ambiguities are reduced to the vanishing point. The problem consists simply in ensuring that the variant spellings of each name are correctly grouped.

Often the situation is similar when dealing with the records found in census schedules. Since most people live in families, there are normally several names in each record, and if another census is taken in five or ten years time, it may be possible to find a matching record in which many of the same names occur, augmented by intervening births and depleted by deaths or by the departure of some members of the family from the parental hearth. But in any such comparison of records from two or more censuses there will also be cases which illustrate a new range of teasing difficulties and involve more than the standardization of names if records are to be linked accurately. For there will always be some young men and women between the dates of any two censuses who leave their parents' home in order to found families themselves. If James Baldwin married in 1855, he is unlikely to be found in 1861 living still with his parents, brothers and sisters as in 1851. If he is still in the same enumeration district he will probably be the head of a separate household, and his name alone may well be insufficient to decide which records should be linked. If Baldwin was a common local name there may be several possibilities between which to decide. Choosing one in preference to another may mean considering other information fields in each record. The longer the interval between any two censuses, the higher the proportion of links which will require more than names alone to be taken into account.

There are analogous problems with vital registration in parish registers. For example, in England it is rare to find a parish register with as much detail as is found in the better French registers. Many records contain only the names of the principal and this may often prove insufficient to identify him unambiguously. This entails resort to more complex testing before a link is made.[5] With registers of this type, therefore, just as with a proportion of census records, the standardization of names, though a necessary preliminary, is only a first step towards the resolution of ambiguities in record linkage.

In these circumstances it will be necessary to turn to other information besides the names in an attempt to solve linkage ambiguities. Age information can be invaluable if it is accurately stated since it narrows down the search area within which to look for a linkable record. For example, if a man at his burial is said to be 35 years old, many baptism records which would otherwise be linkable to the burial may be excluded from consideration. Age information, like name information, provides in principle an unchanging point of reference. The date of any record on which the age of a man is given less his age should always indicate the same year of birth as that obtained similarly from any other record referring to him on which age is stated. And the same is true of some other types of information, notably birthplace.

But there is often other information in nominal records which must be treated much more circumspectly. Both a man's occupation and his place of residence are often given in such records, but they may change considerably during his lifetime so that disagreement in these particulars between any two records must not normally be a bar to their linkage. Problems of this sort are discussed at some length in

[5] This question is discussed more fully in chapter 4.

three of the chapters in this book,[6] together with the associated problems of matchscoring.

Matchscoring is necessary when a choice has to be made between two or more links which remain in conflict with each other after the formation of links has been completed. Not all links are equally strong and this fact can be exploited in simplifying the linkage situation by deleting the weaker links until conflicts no longer exist. In this connection the system used in allocating weights to each link is clearly crucial since it will determine which links are favoured and which broken. There must also be provision in matchscoring for dealing with cases in which there are two or more links or sets of links which score equally highly, and which therefore cannot be resolved simply by preferring the stronger.

SOURCES AND OPPORTUNITIES

In discussing record linkage it is convenient to illustrate the problems which arise by referring to vital registration records or census schedules because more attention has been given to them for this purpose than to other sets of records. But this is only a matter of convenience. In principle the same or analogous opportunities and problems must arise when using any sources in which individuals are named. Indeed more generally it can be argued that historical records of any type, and not just nominal records must obey the same logic.[7]

Nominal records grew more abundant during the sixteenth century in England and thereafter there is a gathering volume of records for the average man until by the twentieth century the filling in of forms has become one of the minor nuisances of life and individual nominal records relating to one man produced in the course of a typical lifetime are numbered by the hundred.

Even in the early modern period nominal records were becoming common—records of baptism, marriage and burial, Poor Law payment and assessment records, settlement papers, churchwarden's accounts, apprenticeship records, wills, tax records, leases, conveyances, extents, enclosure awards. The list could be greatly extended. Between them such records ensured that few men lived out their lives without leaving evidence of their existence in written nominal records. Many appeared in several different types of record.

The hazards of time have destroyed many records, but in some parishes good fortune has secured the survival of a great part of the

---

[6] Those by Winchester, Wrigley and Schofield, and Skolnick.
[7] Winchester pursues this point in chapter 1.

original wealth of documentation. In these parishes much can be added to the skeleton of a man's life provided by the parish register, and the interplay of external circumstances upon the individual and the family can be traced out. How was property and other wealth divided up between offspring as one generation was replaced by the next? Are there notable differences in marriage patterns between families with land and those without? Was the holding of village office confined to a small group of families or widely spread through the community? Was the size of a family's holding varied to meet family needs, or was it invariant, and to complement this were there ways in which the size of the household was kept almost constant to provide the labour needed to exploit the holding fully?[8] Did the type or scale of social mobility change over the centuries? Is it true that enclosure brought with it great changes in the social structure of the village? Did the Speenhamland system encourage early marriage and feckless fertility?

In the nineteenth century a new major base of nominal information covering the whole population became available in countries which conducted censuses based on individual schedules for each household. Record linkage between censuses can provide articulated information comparable to that which can be coaxed out of parish registers at an earlier date. And new record sources came into existence to add to the old in supplementing census schedules—city and trade directories, newspapers, club and union records, records of charitable and benevolent societies, school registers, tax assessments of new types, and so on. The range of investigation which may be undertaken grows wider until the distinction between the traditional preoccupations of history and those of sociology and anthropology narrows considerably.

Just as a logic of linkage may be defined for records drawn from within any given source (for example, for links between baptisms, marriages and burials in parish registers), so too in merging information about individuals from records drawn from two or more different record sources, requirements for linkage can be defined. And, whether the records come from a single source or several, linkage may either involve the consideration of names alone, or of other information fields as well. Indeed, the linkage logic is little affected by the number

[8] The former strategy is reflected in the diary of the Essex clergyman, Ralph Josselin. The latter was prevalent in much of continental Europe. See A. Macfarlane, *The family life of Ralph Josselin, a seventeenth century clergyman: An essay in historical anthropology* (Cambridge, 1970), and for an Austrian example at the opposite end of the spectrum, L. Berkner, 'The stem family and the developmental cycle of the peasant household: an eighteenth century Austrian example', *American Historical Review*, 77 (1972), 398–418.

of sources involved, since it depends essentially upon the information content of the pairs of records concerned.

BIAS AND SAMPLING

All the operations which have been described—whether of standardizing names, searching for and testing potential links between records, or assigning weights to the links and matchscoring and deleting them where necessary—can be performed either by hand or by computer program. Whether it is sensible to use a computer or not will depend on the size of the files of records involved and the likelihood that the program can be used repeatedly on similar files. If the decision lies in favour of the computer, there are several dos and don'ts to be observed in preparing, punching, editing and structuring the data for manipulation by computer. These are touched on in passing in this book and took up much time at the Princeton conference. But the logic of the operations remains identical whether the work is carried out by hand or by machine.[9]

In both cases, though, there may be grave difficulty about the representativeness of the data. No method of data handling and analysis, however sophisticated, can manufacture the empirical data on which it is supposed to feed. Defects in data can take many forms. Some are obvious as, for example, when there is a paucity of identifying characteristics in the records. Others, though equally important, are easily lost to view. In particular there is the problem of bias, omnipresent but often elusive. This, too, took up much discussion time at the conference.[10]

In every source of information there will be bias. Ecclesiastical parish registers are denominational. Non-Anglicans in England, non-Catholics in France will either be missing or under-represented in parish registers. Tax registers either ignore those too poor to pay tax, or, if they are listed, tend to cover that part of the population less fully. Difference of literacy, sex, marital status, age, and length of residence may all produce differential cover even in sources which purport to cover the whole population. In general the poor, the highly mobile and the very young tend to escape recording. In addition there may be many other reasons to suspect that patterns observable in the part of the population made visible by the record source

[9] It does not follow from this that everything can be done by program. This is especially true of name standardization because early spelling was so idiosyncratic. See the appendix to chapter 4 below.
[10] Herlihy devotes a part of his chapter to this issue. See pp. 51–6 below.

may not hold good for the rest. And even if the population were fully covered by a given source, there would be a strong likelihood that any linkage process would introduce bias since the immobile are easier to trace than the mobile and certain parts of the life cycle (partly but not solely for this reason) present greater difficulties for linkage than others.

For example, if the record source is a pair of successive censuses, a man of young adult years with a settled family at the earlier census will be easier to trace in the later census than his younger brother who marries between the two dates, leaving his father's household and setting up one of his own. Similarly, it is a well-known drawback of family reconstitution as a method of investigating the demography of past populations that many of the fertility, mortality and nuptiality rates which can be calculated will refer only to a minority of the population. Only very rarely, and for limited groups, is there firm ground for confidence that coverage is complete.

For this reason much thought should be given to the most effective ways of estimating the nature and extent of the bias present in the basic data or introduced by the process of record linkage. There are a number of straightforward methods of doing this. For example, in family reconstitution if occupation of groom is given at marriage the relative frequencies of different occupations may be calculated from the marriage registers. If these differ substantially from the relative frequencies of completed families tabulated by father's occupation (which would happen if, say, more frequent migration tended to cause labourers' families to be under-represented), there is immediate reason to doubt whether the statistics of such measurements as completed family size for the sample of families tabulated is representative of the whole population.

Where bias can be estimated it is usually possible to make some estimate of its importance, and often feasible to make special studies designed to reduce the uncertainty. Bias, however, may be suspected and yet very difficult to measure, as would be the case in the example given if occupation were not stated at marriage. It is therefore important that any study based on nominal record linkage should discuss the sources of possible bias at some length.

Closely connected with this issue is that of sampling. In detailed studies of small communities, like the parish, a religious sect, or an elite, populations are not large enough for there to be any question of sampling, but vital registers or census schedules covering large populations imply heavy costs in data punching and in producing clean data files. At some point the benefit to be gained from increasing the sample size will not match the marginal cost of processing the data. At that point, whose location will depend on the aims of the particular study, it is inefficient to continue to consider the whole population, and preferable to use an appropriate sampling method to keep the volume of data within bounds.

The general range of choice open to an historian who wishes to cut down the scale of his analysis by sampling has been discussed elsewhere by one of the authors of this volume.[11] Where record linkage is used, special care may be needed in selecting an appropriate method. It would be pointless, for example, to select, say, a 1 in 10 random sample of households in the 1851 and 1861 censuses and then hope to make many intercensal record links since the chance of a household selected in one sample being selected also in the other is very small. Since linkage searches are made within surname sets only, it is essential to ensure that surnames present in one sample are to be found in the other when linking between them. Equally, those not found in one should be excluded from the other. A simple method of achieving this is to sample by including only those with surnames beginning with certain letters of the alphabet. But this is, of course, pointless if surnames themselves change during the course of a lifetime. In England where a woman's surname changes at marriage, this happened to almost half the population reaching adult years. Therefore when sampling for record linkage using vital registers it may be best to consider only individuals who were partners or children in marriages in which both the surname of the groom and the maiden name of the bride begin, say A–M. And even then re-marriage will cause difficulties.

TRUE AND FALSE LINKS

The difficulty of knowing whether a link is true or not underlies all others. A set of rules for making, confirming and rejecting links can be framed and then implemented consistently either by hand or by machine. But the results can just as well be to produce consistent mistakes as consistent correct linkages.

Perfect accuracy is beyond attainment in historical record linkage. The Princeton conference heard[12] of the lengths to which it is

[11] R. S. Schofield, 'Sampling in historical research', in E. A. Wrigley (ed.), *Nineteenth century society: Essays in the use of quantitative methods for the study of social data* (Cambridge, 1972).

[12] From Magnus Magnusson of the Computing Centre, University of Iceland, who contributed a paper entitled, 'Computer methods for the linkage of the National Register, birth records, death records and blood group records in Iceland'.

sometimes necessary to go to secure accuracy even in a small, highly educated modern community with a bureaucracy concerned to secure correct identification. In Iceland, where an interest in genetic and medical questions has led to a large record linkage project covering every Icelander born in this century, it has still proved necessary at times to use the telephone to resolve by direct enquiry ambiguities not soluble from the records alone. Since the information available about any one man in each record is fixed, and may be insufficient to identify him uniquely, and since the dead cannot be interrogated like the living, there will always be doubtful cases in historical record linkage. Furthermore, there will be cases where there is no apparent doubt (because only two records exist which can be linked and the link passes the various rules for linkage), but where the link is yet false, chance coincidence in names and other characteristics having produced a spurious link.

Certain checks upon linkage accuracy are usually possible from within one data source,[13] and still more when there are two or more independent sources. For example, wills may serve to check the completeness and accuracy of family reconstitution in that they often rehearse the living members of a family at a point in time. But there is room both for further discussion of the problem as a whole and for more experiment. One promising approach is to work backwards from a set of truly linked records, which may be generated *ad hoc* or represent a body of data which is known to be reliable, decomposing it into its constituent unlinked records, and then discover how accurately alternative linkage strategies perform, using either all the information fields in the constituent records or only a selection of them to simulate variations in the fullness of recording.

Record linkage work using historical materials largely conforms to the dictum *plus ça change, plus c'est la même chose*. It involves nothing which is offensive to commonsense or traditional practice. As a technique it offers hope of achieving both fuller description of social function and change in the past and more discriminating analysis. But this is secured by extending and formalizing methods which have been familiar since written records were first used for the study of the past, and attempts were made to draw together items of information about particular men or institutions. This is obviously true of the piecing together of fragmentary information about individual lives.

[13] See, for example, E. A. Wrigley (ed.), *An introduction to English historical demography* (London, 1966), p. 158, n. 55.

But, more generally, the selection and ordering of historical accounts has close analogies in record linkage. For example, discrepancies between different accounts of a particular incident are very similar to a linkage situation in which several records are interlinked in ways which are not compatible with each other. In the latter case, the various combinations of links which are mutually compatible are enumerated, the strength of each such combination is considered, and the 'best' solution retained. In the same way, in the former case, the possible accounts of an incident which are internally consistent can be detailed and a choice made between them, preserving the most plausible account at the expense of the others.

When nominal records are both homogeneous and numerous it proves useful to develop formal and often complex operational rules to exploit them to the best advantage. This explains why it is profitable to consider mathematical treatments of similar problems, and also points to the use of computers. The same has happened in sociology and social anthropology in similar circumstances. Such developments are salutary and stimulating because they enforce more rigorous examination of the bases of decision. But those who have mastered the new techniques will continue to be caught up in attempts to answer old questions. When Leeuwenhoek peered down his microscope at water droplets he saw great numbers of animalcules which were invisible to the naked eye. The new record linkage techniques may serve to bring some things into sharper focus and enable them to be viewed in greater detail, but they do not reveal new objects of study. Records of the lives of individual men and women form the basis of all such work, and the upshot of successful record linkage studies is a better understanding of their habits and actions.

Ian Winchester

1   On referring to ordinary historical persons

My purpose in these pages is to draw attention to the fundamental place of record linkage in history: fundamental both in theory and in practice. I will argue that historical reference, i.e. referring to individuals in the past and trying to identify them, cannot be understood without consideration of the notion of record linkage. From this claim, if it stands, it follows that historical existence claims, historical predicate corroboration and the growth of historical knowledge in general, presuppose historical record linkage. In a manner analogous to that in which mathematics is a certain kind of speculation controlled by proof, history is then seen to be speculation about the past controlled by record linkage operations.

I would like to begin with the commonsense view of what it is to make a correct historical reference. Most of us would agree that in our everyday lives we generate various records pertaining to our existence which might be passed down to future generations after we are dead and buried. If we are famous, sinful or plain unlucky, or if we write a lot of letters, we are quite likely to appear in newspapers. In this event, at the very least we will leave behind as a trace of ourselves a name, probably an age at a certain date, perhaps our profession at that time, one or two other bits of personal information, such as whether or not we are married, and finally the details of the event which led to the newspaper story. What enables this information to be said truly to pick out, to individuate just this or that one among us, is that the information be both accurate and sufficiently discriminating that no other person is selected as well. Perhaps we all take it for granted that such information, with sufficient care, *could* be got right by newspaper reporters dealing with living people, even if in fact this rarely happens. And the reason that we think that it could be got right is that the individual referred to could be approached and asked, or, failing him, at least a friend or other individual who knew him intimately. That is, in the case of a living human being there is the possibility, at least, of setting the record straight by re-identification of that individual.

It is a very short step, a very short analogical step, to go from the records generated by a man who is living to the records generated by a man who has just had a fatal coronary. Given the general conceptual scheme within which we operate, which involves men of all ages, being born, living and doing things, and in their death throes and beyond, we have no difficulty in accepting the fact that these records *were* generated by a once living man. That we can for living men re-identify them is, it seems, sufficient for us not to worry about the fact that we can no longer re-identify dead men in the same way. Even if a man is dead, we can sometimes ask his relatives and friends about what he was like. And even if all of his relatives and friends are dead, we can always compare records pertaining to him, or seeming to pertain to him, to ascertain the truth.

So for us historical reference in the sense of reference to once living persons is no mystery, but a commonplace. Yet, as might be expected, there are certain differences in the logic we employ when faced with records pertaining to dead people. For example, for living persons involved in libel suits it is necessary to establish exactly what was written, when, by whom, and with what intention. It is necessary for us to be able, that is, to identify an author of certain words or certain parts of contemporary records. And a vital part of this process will certainly be the existence of the author in question, and of his handiness as a referent. In general, we believe that in such cases the truth can be ascertained.

Of course for dead persons libel cannot arise, for we cannot try the dead. But more important, we cannot ask the dead to help us establish identity either. So for identification of the dead we are entirely dependent upon other living persons, or upon records, or upon both at the same time. In some of the most interesting cases involving historical reference (such as in the matter of Hitler's death) we are entirely dependent upon records. Perhaps for this very reason the matter is controversial. Yet, most of us are convinced that somehow, somewhere in those records, the truth lies. And anyway, even if it doesn't lie in the records, it exists (perhaps in a Platonic heaven) even if we cannot aspire to it.

In such cases we are very naturally led to probability statements. And we are so led simply because we cannot, in any way available to us, determine what is true. Yet we are quite certain that some set of statements or other is true. Now I have slipped over from talking about identifying historical persons to ascertaining the truth about historical events. Yet it seems clear that the latter is logically tied to the former.

If, in attempting successfully to identify a historical individual, we are forced to consider a record or records drawn from files of other similar records, then we may find ourselves in one of the following situations:

1   we have an individual in mind whose record(s) we are searching after
2   we are searching for an individual who displays certain characteristics in which we are already interested
3   we are really just riffling through the files hoping to turn up something interesting, in terms of some rather general criteria.

Clearly, if we have an already famous historical personage in mind, such as Napoleon or Wellington or Hitler, we are engaged in the first sort of search. If we are an economic historian looking for the financial standing of ordinary Victorians we might be engaged in the second. And if we are a more broadly-based social historian, looking through files of records for patterns, patterns as yet unknown, we might be engaged in the third.

Any of these three inquiries presupposes that the record files in question were actually generated at some historical time and place by people who were once living. Hence our inquiry presupposes that we can already identify the class of persons without difficulty. In searching for a particular triangle you must already know what a triangle is. In searching for a particular person you must already know what a person is; and this latter holds just as well in the search for historical persons.

In all files of records which were generated at one historical time, certain prerequisites must be fulfilled, if they are to be used in later ages to identify or individuate a particular historical person. First and foremost among these is that such records must contain items of information *about* or pertaining to the historical individual who is to be identified. Without any such items, clearly such a record is of no use. Such items as can be used to individuate historical persons can conveniently be referred to as *identifying items*. Such items may span an enormous range of matters pertaining to a man's life. The most obvious, of course, is the name of the individual in question. Other such items are his sex (which may be derived from the name as a rule, but may not in such cases as George Sand and George Eliot), his age at a particular date, his income, or any ordinary or extraordinary feat performed (for example, 'defeated Napoleon at Waterloo'), and so on.

How such identifying items are actually employed by the historian depends upon what search-type the historian has in mind. It is obvious that the so-called identifying items in themselves are neutral as to their employment. For it may be of equal interest to an historian to know how many Russells and Smiths there were in the mid-nineteenth century with such and such a yearly income as it is to know that this particular Russell was the grandfather of Bertrand Russell. This is not to deny that certain identifying items are more helpful than others in the individuating process. Criteria can easily be established as to the relative merit of a particular class of items compared with another class, for purposes of historical individuation. Just as in individuating among living persons we are likely to choose characteristics known to be present in the same individual over a long period of time ('he is called Quigley Albert', 'his fingerprint pattern is . . .', 'she has a mole on her left buttock', 'her temper is uncontrollable'), so in individuating among historical persons we are likely to select as identifying items those which tend to be present from record to record as being the best for such purposes (newspapers, for example, generally give name, age, rank, station or occupation, marital status, and major accomplishment if any).

Here, however, a major difference between the logic of individuating among living persons and the logic of individuating among historical persons shows itself. For in the case of living persons there is always, at least in principle, the opportunity of increasing the discriminating predicates *ad infinitum*. But historical persons, identified as they are by their records, leave behind but a finite number of applicable predicates or identifying items. Whereas for living individuals we can always meet the demand for more and more identifying items, we cannot do the same for historical individuals. For the number of records on the earth is finite. And the number of identifying items contained on such records is also finite. Hence historical identification of an historical individual, is a matter of discrimination based upon a finite number of identifiers.

Part of the reason that the identification of living individuals can be positive, certain and non-probabilistic—at least in very many cases, is that we can always increase the number of identifying items at will. On the other hand, while of course historical identification *can* certainly succeed, there is still the very important logical difference that we cannot do the same even in principle. We are invariably stuck with just the set of identifying items present on a record or set of records being used to make an identifying reference. This means that historical identification is intrinsically probabilistic.

To establish this latter claim will require a little more argument and a little technicality. It is perhaps clear to the reader that I have a particular *model* of historical individuation in mind, and that what I have been saying presupposes that particular model. Hence if what I say is wrong in whole or part, it is probably because the model of historical identification which I am employing is inadequate to serve as the paradigm of all historical identification, of all individuating reference to historical persons, and ultimately of historical individuals in general. And there is one other question which must be aired, that is the question of when we are to say that we have accomplished an historical identification. Does identifying an historical individual entail re-identification? In the case of a living person, to have succeeded in identifying him, amounts to having succeeded in re-identifying him. For to become acquainted with a living person for the very first time is not to have *identified* him, but rather, to have met him. Hence to identify is to have already certain predicates in mind, to think or act identifyingly is to think or act re-identifyingly. For us, concerned as we are with the identification of historical persons, must we re-identify a historical individual in order to succeed in identifying him? First, then, what is my model, and what amounts to identification with respect to that model?

THE RECORD LINKAGE MODEL OF HISTORICAL INDIVIDUATION

By a *record* I mean, in general, any particular material object produced due to the presence of a once living person, which would not have been produced, had that person not lived. In ordinary historical circumstances such records are likely to take the form of letters, wills, documents of all sorts, birth, marriage and death records, newspaper items, census and assessment documents, drivers' licences, hospital admission slips, credit cards and so on. However, clothing, personal possessions, commissioned pictures, photographs and many others also fall within this definition of a record.

In order for a record to be a *potentially identifying record*, it must contain data which can be used as *identifying items*. That is, it must contain a predicate or predicates which either pertained to a particular living human being or were thought to do so. In this class of predicates comes the fingerprints on a police record, the national health number on a hospital admission slip, the name, age, sex, occupation on census and assessment rolls, and so on. Here I make no assumptions that the predicates on the record must actually have been true predicates of the individual of whom they were at one time recorded *as* true predicates. The reason for this lack of restriction is twofold. In individuating living human beings we never have more than predicates which are *taken* to be true of that individual for individuating purposes. Hence we cannot, in fairness, be more stringent upon historical persons in this respect. The second reason is that commonly in historical practice identifying items of the sort mentioned are often discrepant between truly linked pairs of record. This is analogous to a policeman filling out four copies of a warrant of arrest with spelling variations in the surname and with minor discrepancies in the other identifying information (for example, age, occupation) on the warrant copies, taken pair by pair. It might be argued that such occurrences are 'mistakes' and must not be allowed into any theory of historical reference. But anyone arguing thus doesn't realize the difference between mistakes and discrepancies. I may say of a particular person that she has auburn hair, and another may say that she has brown hair. Or I may say of a man that he is a cabinet-maker, and another may say that he is a shipbuilder. This ambiguity of description is not an unfortunate lack of scientific precision, but rather a fact of language which any theory of reference must take into account. A man may be referred to by his fellow as 'John', 'Jim', and 'Red'. To ask which is his *true* proper name is to ask an absurd question, unless what was intended was to ask by what name he was baptized, which is quite different.

Historical individuation, according to my model, consists in bringing together pairs of records pertaining to historical individuals, and comparing certain items on such records as to their agreement or disagreement, when the items are present on both records. In the event that all, or at any rate a sufficient number of the identifying items on a particular pair of records are in agreement, the historian may then judge that a historical individuation has been successfully brought about. The question as to what constitutes a 'sufficient number' of identifying items in agreement is a question for the historian's personal judgement. However, in aiding such judgement certain probability considerations may be brought to bear. Indeed, the historian may often bring these to his aid when he applies his mysterious 'judgement'. There are two sorts of probability considerations which a historian might bring to bear. The first might be roughly characterized as involving general background knowledge; the second characterized as knowledge of his specific record files. When the historian guesses that the person on record A, namely John Smith, Tailor, is the very same person who generated record B where he is recorded as John Smith, Sailor, he is applying his background knowledge concerning the similarity in written latin script between 'T' and 'S'. Were he to add that in this particular file pair upon which he had been working for some time the scribes often wrote their capital 'S' and 'T' indistinguishably, he would be applying a probability consideration derived from a knowledge of his specific files. If he characterized this numerically as being two times out of three he would be well on the way to assigning a probability number to his judgement, derived jointly from his background knowledge and from a knowledge of his specific files. Of course this latter knowledge may not be based specifically on any frequency counts. What is important is that individuation in this sense is intrinsically probabilistic, due to the fact that the number of identifying items is small and finite, and that discrepancies on truly linked pairs of records, for *all* identifying item kinds are a historical fact of life.

Let us pause for a moment over the apparent circularity involved in the notion of 'truly linked pairs' as portrayed above. The difficulty is this. We are claiming that historical individuation brought about by a record linkage process is intrinsically probabilistic since the number of identifying items is finite and since they are liable to discrepancy. On the other hand, we would like to refer to pairs of *truly* linked records. Are we ever entitled to think that we have a pair or a collection of pairs of *truly* linked records?

There are three separate questions which need to be distinguished here. The first is whether or not there really are, in ordinary historical practice, truly linked pairs of records. The second is whether we are ever *certain*, in a particular case, that a particular pair of records is truly linked. And third is whether or not, given an entire file of record pairs linked by a man (or perhaps by a machine), we are ever certain that the entire file consists solely of truly linked record pairs.

As regards the first question, concerning the existence of truly linked pairs, the answer is undeniably yes, since daily we generate them ourselves. Moreover, we are very often in a situation with our individual record pairs where we have no doubt about their accuracy. For example, if I receive two letters from Cambridge, England with identical letterheads, and if each letter is composed in the same style and signed by the same man in exactly the same manner, then I am completely certain that both of these letters came from him. Of course this is not to deny the logical possibility that two different people composed these letters or that a typewriter and a pen in a fit of boredom collaborated on the job with no human assistance. But certainty is related to practical possibility not to logical possibility. So in ordinary historical practice, just as in everyday life, there exist truly linked record pairs, and we are often certain in a particular case that a pair of records is truly linked.

The third question, namely, whether or not for an entire file of records linked by a human being or a machine we are ever certain that the file as a whole consists of truly linked pairs, is considerably more complex and difficult. At this point in the interest of clarity I shall use an example drawn from my experience with the Hamilton Project[1] and the many kinds of records linkages with which our group is concerned. In the course of one of our record linkage operations involving a census roll and an assessment roll made in the same city within three months of one another, we created a file of records consisting of 1955 record pairs which we considered to be 'truly linked'. Our object was to see if, by computer, we could simulate the operations of the person who linked the file pair by hand and produce a computer linked file consisting of the same record pairs.

The first rule which was employed by us in generating the 1955 truly linked pairs was this:

> If there is one and only one record in file A with a particular set of identifying items and one and only one record in file B with an identical set of identifying items then we consider that the records refer to one and the same historical individual.

This amounts to the same thing as the principle that if two individuals referred to are characterized by identical predicates then the individuals themselves are identical. Clearly, this principle is only adequate when there are not multiple records in each file with identical identifying items sets. This principle and this qualification involve, if extended to an unlimited number of identifying predicates, the classical principle of the Identity of Indiscernibles and the classical objection to it as a universal logical principle. In slightly more formal terms we might express this principle as:

---

[1] The Hamilton Project (now the Canadian Social History Project) is a research group of the Ontario Institute for Studies in Education. Its object is to study the social structure of a Canadian city undergoing rapid change from an agricultural to a heavy industrial base in the mid-nineteenth century.

If for any predicate of an individual A there corresponds an identical predicate for an individual B such that, as regards identifying predicates there is no way of distinguishing between A and B, then A and B are identical.

And more formally still

$$(\phi)(\phi A = \phi B) \rightarrow A = B$$

Now we can characterize all of the further moves made in generating our 'truly linked' file in terms of attempts to maintain this principle in the face of empirical difficulties by means of ingenious excuses based on background knowledge.

Thus, for example, if we found a record in file A with the name 'John Smith' inscribed and a record in file B with the name 'John Smythe', and if there were no other Smiths or Smythes in either file, we then upheld the principle by claiming that although the identifying items 'Smith' and 'Smythe' are not visually identical they are phonetically identical. This means that we maintain our rule here by claiming that

$$\phi A = \phi B \text{ (Phi of } A \text{ is the same sound as Phi of } B)$$
$$\text{sound}$$

in this case

$$(\text{Smith})A = (\text{Smythe})B$$
$$\text{sound}$$

A similar sort of explaining away of apparent discrepancies was employed for the rest of our 'truly linked' file of pairs. Thus, for example, if one Abraham P. Appleby, aged 17 is present in file A and one Abraham P. Appleby aged 71 is present in file B then background knowledge concerning the possibility that numbers get reversed in transcription, and the fact that our 17 year old Abraham Appleby has three sons and two grandsons are invoked. This amounts to a maintenance of the Identity of Indiscernibles principle in that we admit the number string 1,7 to be identical to the number string 7,1 when order of the numbers is not considered. Thus in this case we have

$$(1,7)A = (7,1)B$$
$$\text{non-ordered}$$
$$\text{number pairs}$$

This is not to deny that we employ the background knowledge in order to arrive at the excuse and hence the looser criterion of identity of predicates. But, formally we maintain the principle of the Identity of Indiscernibles by explaining away an apparently discernible predicate pair as not discernible at another level.[2]

In the cases in which there were multiple candidates in one or both files for linkage with identical identifying predicate sets or in which identifying items are discrepant and no reasonable excuse can be found, either the linkage decision was suspended or a non-linkage declared.

This returns us to our third question, namely, have we ever any reason to believe that we are in possession of a file consisting entirely of 'truly linked' pairs of records? Our answer can be straightforward, if tentative. If we have reason to believe that the Identity of Indiscernibles in its finite form is an applicable principle to invoke and the 'excuse procedure' is an acceptable one, then it is possible that we might generate an entire file of records consisting solely of truly linked pairs. Provided we are willing to be conservative in the records we consider to be linked we can be as certain as we like that all the records in our linked file are 'truly linked pairs'. However, we are never in such a position that we can prove by some means *more* fundamental than the Identity of Indiscernibles and an 'excuse procedure' that all of the records in our file of linked pairs are truly linked and that we have identified the total number of linked pairs common to the original files. This means that the logical possibility always exists that there might be more truly linked pairs which we have not found and that in our file of identified pairs there are some which are not, in fact, truly linked. This logical possibility may be of serious concern under some circumstances and of no concern at all under others. It is possible to imagine circumstances under which the

---

[2] A careful reader of the published material on the Hamilton Project or of the work of H. B. Newcombe will discover that the employment of a version of the Identity of Indiscernibles and the explaining away of apparent discrepancies is fundamental to the process of generating the so-called 'truly linked pairs'. Some writers, notably Felligi and Sunter, although their record linkage model assumes the existence of 'truly linked pairs' nonetheless shy away in practice from any procedure for generating such pairs in order to estimate weights for agreements and disagreements in identifying items. By invoking an independence assumption they develop a method of getting a statistically 'best' solution to any record linkage problem involving two files of records by using error estimates from frequency counts of the identifying items in the files. See I. Winchester 'Record linkage techniques', *Journal of Interdisciplinary History*, I (1970), 107–24; H. B. Newcombe and J. M. Kennedy, 'Making maximum use of the discriminating power of identifying information', *Communications of the Association for Computing Machinery*, V (1962), 563–6; I. P. Felligi and A. B. Sunter, 'A theory for record linkage', *Journal of the American Statistical Association*, 64 (1969), 1183–1210.

Identity of Indiscernibles principle is only weakly applicable, if applicable at all. For example, if every record in a file had at least one companion with an identical identifying item set, or if every potential pair of linked records between a file pair contained apparently discrepant items, we would be in a state of absolute doubt about every linkage we generated, whatever rule we employed. Happily, such situations do not arise in real life historical settings.

It is possible to doubt the applicability of the Identity of Indiscernibles principle. But the only serious objection to the principle which has so far been raised by philosophers is with respect to the question of spatio-temporal location of a particular. Some philosophers are inclined to hold that if individuals A and B agree in all other predicates it is still possible for them to be non-identical in that they might be located differently in space at one and the same time. For a historian, spatio-temporal location is itself an identifying item. Consequently this objection is not available to the historian. I will hence conclude that this is the principle which historians in fact employ in ordinary record linkage contexts. It does not follow that it is the principle which they ought to employ. However, since I know of no alternatives (although I do not know of a proof that there are none), it may very well be the only possible principle presupposed in record linkage via identifying items. If this is so, it must count as a very fundamental principle for history.

That, then, is the model. But what of the other problem that was raised earlier? I have spoken boldly, when describing the model, about historical individuation being achieved by bringing together pairs of records, each pair supposed to have been generated by one historical individual. Why pairs of such record? Why not only one record? Why not 10 records? Why not 100? The reason that I have spoken in this manner is that history thrives on corroborated events, or on corroborated predicates applying to particular historical individuals. And a minimum version of corroboration is a pair of linked records with the same descriptive item on each.

This is closely connected with the puzzle concerning the identification and re-identification of living individuals. For if it is true that in the case of living individuals to identify an individual is to re-identify an individual, then how much more true must this dictum be in the case of historical individuals. To have turned up a solitary record on an individual that you have never met, seen or heard before cannot count as having *identified* an historical individual. At this point, it seems, one has just met the record. And if we leave the record, go to the dining room, and then pick it up again we have now certainly re-identified something. But in this case it is only the record, not the historical individual. We have still no more than a collection of predicates, of potential identifying items, in our hands.

There are two cases which seem to present some difficulty to this line of argument, namely, the case of the possession of an entire file of records (say a census file) and the case of a single record which (say a will or history book) might be analysed into a number of separate previous instances of record linkage operations. In the case of the file of records we seem to have the right to say, right away, that every individual in this file exists (or did exist). Is this not equivalent to saying that we have identified each individual? And have we not the right to affirm in each individual case, the predicates we find associated with the individual? I think the answer here is that the distinction between affirming that for every individual *place* in a file of records there corresponds an individual who lives (or lived) and affirming that a particular individual *A* is the *very same* individual as the individual *B*, is about as great a distinction as can be. Roughly, it is the distinction between 'a man' and 'the man'. With respect to the predicates we are entitled to affirm, that if the records were carefully recorded and we know they were, then more often than not the information is correct. But in each individual case, unless we possess special knowledge about the manner of the recording (such as that in these police files everything is quadruple checked), we have un-corroborated information. Such information is very useful for statistical work on the assumption that things are more often gotten right than wrong. But to use it to characterize one of the individuals in the file prior to linkage is, it seems, to say something uncorroborated about somebody unknown; more accurately, it is to say something neither likely nor unlikely about someone neither known nor un-known.

There is another way of looking at a case of a file of records. We might consider them to be already linked with respect to such un-spoken items as location in time and place or with respect to some other item. For example records in a list of Lion's Club members from 1925 in Cambridge, England all have a certain number of items in common, which is why they form a file. In this sense we can say that member *A* and member *B* are linked according to club member-ship, etc. Is this sort of linkage sufficient to enable us to say that the individuals in the club roster are all identified? It is common to distinguish between qualitative identity and numerical identity in logic. To be qualitatively identified is to be picked out as a member of some class or kind of individuals. To be numerically identified is to be individuated, i.e. to be picked out as being the very same individual. In the qualitative sense, the members of the club are all identified in so far as they are all members of the same club. But we still do not know something of the form 'A is the very same individual member of the club as B'.[3] This means that we may consider a historical individual to be identified with respect to some class or kind and still not individuated.

The second case is that of a single record containing a number of identifying predicates and equivalent to a linking of a number of simpler records in time. Now there is a sense in which any record which contains more than one descriptive item pertaining to an individual *could* be considered as consisting of prior linkages of simpler records in time or space. What is important, from the point of view of the historian, is how he comes across the record or records which concern him. A single record without a context to back it up, regardless of the number of identifying items on the record is neither identifying nor individuating. Unless the historian is personally acquainted with the person who generated the record (say a will) or unless he has previous historical knowledge concerning the individual via other records, there is no sense at all in the suggestion that the record could be identifying in the numerical sense.

A minimal version of historical identification in either the qualitative or numerical senses is therefore a linked pair of records. And this is also a minimal version of corroborated predicates. But both the identification procedure and therefore the procedure of predicate corroboration are intrinsically probabilistic because the number of identifying items shared by record pairs is finite and not expansible at will.

I have argued that the notion of historical identification and of historical individuation cannot be understood without an understanding of record linkage processes. There are a number of other philosophical claims which are closely related to this claim which must be examined, together with certain obvious objections to them. The claims are that

1   record linkage, as understood above, is *the* technique fundamental to the establishing of historical existence claims (such as that Socrates existed but Homer did not);
2   record linkage is the technique fundamental to the corroboration

---

[3] Technically, when we can confidently link a record pair we are in a position to claim that the identifying item set on each record is individuating. Prior to this, we do not know that it is so.

of historical predicates (such as that Socrates died in 399 B.C. by his own hand);

3   record linkage is the technique fundamental to the increase of historical knowledge in general.

Now, what are the obvious objections to these claims?

HISTORICAL EXISTENCE CLAIMS

With respect to the view that record linkage is the technique, the one and only technique fundamental to establishing historical existence claims, the following objection leaps to mind. Very often the historian accepts the existence of a particular historical individual with no appeal to record linkage whatever. In particular, a social historian casually looking through a parish register or a census record file or the like certainly does not begin by doubting the past existence of the individuals whose names appear in the files. He accepts them, it seems, straightaway. So here is a clear counter example to my thesis of the primacy of record linkage for establishing and maintaining (or perhaps rejecting) historical existence claims.

This would, however, be a very hasty rejection of my thesis. For whenever a historian looks through a parish register at names, or whenever he goes out to Woodstock to consult the Marlborough archives, or whenever he scans a census file record, a newspaper or a club list, he is looking at records which are already linked with one another by virtue of their relating to one and the same historical individual. For example, the parish records all relate to a particular parish —a perfectly good historical individual, albeit not a person. Or the archive records at Woodstock, to take the second case, all relate to 'the Marlborough family' and are linked to them by virtue of their spatio-temporal location and, perhaps, by identifying items. The same sort of thing can be said for the newspaper, club list and the like.

On the other hand, imagine a historian who happens to be a lover of deserts who comes across a completely context-free record with a person's name on it and a number of predicates supposedly applicable to that person in the midst of one of his favourite deserts. Is the historian entitled to say he has now identified a historical individual and that that individual exists? I think not. However, if he took his record along with him to the nearest town and discovered in the parish register there a man with that name he might feel justified in claiming that the man in question existed.

HISTORICAL PREDICATE CORROBORATION

The claim that record linkage is the fundamental technique underlying historical predicate corroboration seems to me to be obvious and undeniable. How else, but by comparing the predicates on records relating (or apparently relating) to one and the same historical individual can historical predicates be corroborated at all? Thus statements such as 'Hitler died in a bunker in 1945' are subject to debate precisely because the records linked to Hitler's biography are inconclusive on this point. Eyewitness reports and Russian photographs of the body shared immediately with the Allies might have been conclusive. What is important here is having enough records of a sort not easily doubted which link up in the manner in which biographical facts in a parish register or in census and assessment rolls often link up.

An objection which might be made both to the claim that record linkage underlies the establishment of historical existence and to historical predicate corroboration is that records which are truly linked often contain discrepant identifying information. It follows that if we are to use the identifying items as a source of reference to a particular individual, our identifying expressions are necessarily sometimes in error. Worse, where the identifying items fail to agree, are uncorroborated, we have positive evidence to distrust the other descriptive predicates contained in our records as well. And they, since they are not identifying items, are completely uncorroborated.

In our historical work (i.e. the Hamilton Project) we have often been faced with precisely this situation. What we have done is simply to accept one or other of the records as being correct by fiat and created our cross tabulations on that basis. Since our work is quasi-statistical, we can pass off the conclusions that a few incorrect descriptive items here or there do not matter very much. But what can the more conventional historian, the biographer of a parliament or person say? Only that for him there is conflicting evidence on this or that point. And that is all there is to be said.

Of course, there are some cases in which apparent discrepancies in descriptive items turn out to be not discrepancies at all. Thus if we find a record characterizing an individual as a cabinet maker and another characterizing him as a joiner, we are fully justified in using our knowledge of the ways of the world to declare synonymy here.

INCREASE OF HISTORICAL KNOWLEDGE

My third claim was that record linkage is *the* technique underlying the increase of historical knowledge. This requires a little elaboration and qualification. It is clear the predicate collections relating to historical individuals are built up by processes of record linkage. However, historical knowledge is not simply collections of predicates truly ascribed to identified historical individuals. If it were, history would indeed be a process easily turned over to an electro-mechanical historian substitute. Linked records and masses of cross-tabulations, as all historians know, are not history. So the increase in historical knowledge is not simply ascribable to record linkage. But without processes of record linkage the increase of historical knowledge would be strictly impossible. For the essence of historical description consists in the historian being able to say that not only does a particular descriptive phrase 'X' apply to a particular historical individual (person, depression, organization, war) but that another descriptive phrase 'Y' applies as well. But the precondition for applying two descriptive phrases to the same historical individual is that, at some stage two records containing these phrases and relating to the same individual are linked.

Having taken the strong view that record linkage is the fundamental historical technique for individuation, predicate corroboration and the increase of historical knowledge, it is only fair for me to present a paradox which can be illustrated from the Hamilton Project work. It is a trivial paradox, but seems to me to be as bothersome a puzzle for automated record linkage as Russell's class of all classes paradox was to the logicist program. The puzzle arises out of our willingness to admit that a record pair can be truly linked even if they contain discrepant identifying items. It is easy to construct an example of a pair of records which in our formal system we would wish to treat as truly linked, but which are difficult for us to interpret as a genuine case of (a) historical individuation, (b) predicate corroboration or (c) the increase of historical knowledge. For example, consider the following record pair:

Surname	Initials	Birthdate	Birthplace	Occupation
Berkeley	G.J.	1676	Ireland	Tailor
Barclay	J.G.	1667	Dublin	Sailor

In the example, we have surnames which sound the same, initials which are in reversed order, birthdates which contain a digit switch, a birthplace which is equivalent, though discrepant, and an occupation which is discrepant in the initial capital letter which, on a manuscript, might be easily confused. Any good weighting system and program would take into account such discrepancies and assign a high weight to this being a linkage. The puzzle I wish to present is this: whom have we identified? Berkeley or Barclay?

There are two problems correlative with this one. The first is that even if we resolve the question of whom we have identified, we have still to determine what we are entitled to say about the individual identified. This problem arises because we are concerned with a case in which each descriptive item in the record pair contains discrepant terms. Consequently we seem to have either discorroboration of descriptive predicates or, at best, no corroboration. The second correlative problem is that, beyond the identifying items present on the records there may be other descriptive items which are not common to the record pair, and it is not clear whether we ought to treat *them* at their face value as opposed to considering the other discrepancies as good reason to doubt the remaining information as well. There is not space to treat this pair of problems fully here, so I must be content merely to point out the difficulties.

As regards the question of whom we have identified, three possibilities may be considered. The first is arbitrarily to choose one of the names to represent the person identified. The second is to consider that we have identified either Berkeley or Barclay, but not both. And the third is to consider the proper names to be constituents of a singular expression 'the person who was called either Berkeley or Barclay or both'. The arbitrary choosing of one of the names does not seem to be right. This is the sort of move we might make if we wished to cross-tabulate values of descriptive items and we arbitrarily chose the identifying item value on the first record pair. But with proper names it seems to have no point. We could invent a point of course. Perhaps the Berkeleys were noble and the Barclays base. If we wished to tabulate the number of noblemen we would be forced to make a choice here, if this was all we had to go on. The second suggestion, namely, to consider that we have identified Berkeley or Barclay, but not both seems to be logically impossible. For we are assuming that the linkage relation A is linked to B entails $A = B$ and hence we cannot express ourselves this way at all. The most generally correct conclusion seems to be the third, namely, that we are to interpret our linkage as producing the right to employ the singular term 'the person who was called either Berkeley or Barclay or both'. This still leaves room for a quibble over the 'or both' which I will ignore.

Because my conclusion is that we must, at least in this sort of case, give up using proper names straightforwardly and replace them by a guarded identifying phrase, a more general account of proper names in historical contexts seems called for. Bertrand Russell has given a very influential account of proper names which leads to the conclusion that all cases of proper names in historical contexts are cases of disguised descriptions. Is my account of the function of proper names in record linkage contexts consistent with this view? As Russell's rather paradoxical account of proper names cannot be understood without a bit of background I will first sketch this,[4] and then turn to the account of proper names suggested by record linkage.

The historian ought to be concerned not to construct nonsense sentences. At the very least, this seems to require that the historian knows the meaning of every word in his sentence and that the reader of the history is similarly equipped. Suppose that a historian wants to assert something like the following:

G. J. Berkeley, an Irish tailor, was born in 1676

or

J. G. Barclay, a Dublin sailor, was born in 1667

For a long time philosophers held that proper names were the very best examples of names which had the meaning of straightforwardly pointing to their objects. Thus a proper name, correctly used, referred directly to a particular object. If, therefore, the historian does not know the meaning of a name he employs, that is, does not know to whom that name refers, then he cannot understand the sentence he asserts. A historian, therefore, asserting either of the two sentences drawn from our example, would be speaking nonsense, and not merely falsehood. Yet as the logician Frege and as Russell himself recognized, a historian asserting these sentences would not be talking nonsense. The difficulty is to give an account of why this is so without dropping the requirement that a sentence which makes sense must contain nothing but meaningful words. Russell's answer is that the proper name in these sentences is only apparently a proper name. In reality, it is, in fact a disguised description. Frege's answer is that

[4] B. Russell, 'On denoting', *Mind*, 14 (1905), 479–93; B. Russell, 'Knowledge by acquaintance and knowledge by description', in R. C. Marsh (ed.), *Logic and knowledge* (London, 1956).

every name has both a sense and a reference and that in the case of proper names two people may share the reference of the name but need not share the sense. For example, one man may know that 'The Morning Star' refers to Venus and another that 'The Evening Star' refers to Venus. In this case they share the reference. But they might not both know that The Morning Star = The Evening Star. One might and the other might not. And only one might know that both the Morning Star and the Evening Star are the second planet from the sun. 'Sense and reference', mark much the same distinction as 'connotation and denotation'. Frege's answer, however, is less relevant to our problem than Russell's to which I now turn.

According to Russell, if a historian wished to assert that:

Bertrand Russell is the author of the article 'On Denoting' which appeared in *Mind* 1905   (1)

he could only do so without qualification if he was personally acquainted with Russell. If he was not acquainted with Russell, then what he is entitled to assert involves replacing 'Bertrand Russell' with a descriptive phrase such as 'the co-chairman with Jean-Paul Sartre of the War Crimes Tribunal'. This would mean that the historian would, in reality, be entitled to assert something like:

The co-chairman (with Sartre) of the War Crimes Tribunal is the author of the article 'On Denoting' etc,   (2)

If we apply this doctrine to the Berkeley/Barclay case, we find that all the historian is entitled to assert for:

G. J. Berkeley, an Irish tailor, born in 1676   (3)

is a sentence in which the proper name is replaced by a description. Now in many record linkage contexts only a pair of records is available so that the only identifying description which is available would have to come from the other record of a record pair. In this case, we would be entitled to assert something like:

The Irish tailor, born in 1676 is the Dublin sailor, born in 1667   (4)

In one sense, this seems to be consistent and in another it is an obvious contradiction. It is an obvious contradiction if we wish to suggest that the historian is entitled to assert that an Irish tailor, born in 1676 is also a Dublin sailor born 9 years earlier. But it makes sense if what we are entitled to assert is that the man referred to on one occasion by the identifying items of Irish tailorhood and 1676 birth is one and the same man who is referred to on another occasion by the identifying items of Dublin sailorhood and 1667 birth. The effect of Russell's doctrine is to suggest that for purposes of both identification and assertion in historical contexts the proper name is dispensable, while in ordinary contexts in which the identification is made by someone personally acquainted with an individual, the proper name is necessary and indispensable.

Historical practice seems to lead to just the opposite conclusion in the following way. According to Russell, in ordinary contexts the proper name is a unique symbol standing for an individual with whom the referee is acquainted (in the sense of having, felt, heard, seen or smelled the individual in question). Once a person is acquainted with an ordinary individual, identifying that individual is just a matter of calling up the proper name of the individual. However, in Russell's view, in historical contexts, identifying an individual cannot (at least in normal circumstances) consist of calling up a proper name since to do so requires that the historical individual be an acquaintance of the historian. Usually this does not obtain.

In record linkage contexts, however, the proper name often functions as the most important and perhaps as a uniquely identifying item. Russell is of course right that historians are usually unacquainted in the sensual sense with the individuals to whom they refer and whom they identify. On the other hand, this fact does not by itself abrogate their title to employ whatever identifying items they find necessary in order to get on with their business. And, because proper names are often indispensable for identifying purposes, it would seem silly to suggest that historians are not really entitled to employ them in assertions either. Indeed, it is in everyday contexts where we may most easily dispense with proper names and employ less universally effective identifying descriptive items such as 'the largest man in the room' or 'the girl with the red hair' or pronouns such as 'you'. Proper names in such contexts are very reasonably thought of as backed by descriptive phrases which we might call upon when clarification is needed concerning a particular attempted reference. But often in record linkage contexts to think of a proper name as *backed* by descriptive phrases makes no sense since the descriptive items stand on the same footing as the proper name itself. It is only in cases such as Berkeley/Barclay that we are forced to consider a descriptive phrase as being the very best we can assert under the circumstances. And even here it is not as if we had a proper name which was backed by a description. Rather, we are not sure which proper name to employ under the circumstances, so we do the next best thing.

What social historians *do* seems unobjectionable. The employment of proper names for record linkage is often quite indispensable. So we may turn to the related question: What can philosophers learn from the social historians? In particular, what is the function of the proper name in a record linkage context? Or has the proper name many functions? Does the proper name compete with other items, descriptive items, in record linkage contexts (as philosophers seem to consider) or does it perform a supplementary role?

KINDS OF RECORD LINKAGE

Record linkage as it is practised in present day social history is of two main kinds, family record linkage and personal record linkage. The former kind is that involved in family reconstitution. The latter is that involved in the bringing together of records drawn from disparate routinely gathered files of records such as census or assessment role files, all pertaining to the same individual person.

In the first kind of record linkage it is important to note that the records derived from, for example, a parish register are already pre-linked to a certain extent. They are all linked according to locale, to parish. Further they are all linked according to a certain range of dates. In order to build up a file of family records the main identifying item for this purpose is the family surname. The supplementary identifying items are kind and date of vital event: marriage, birth, death. Essentially the linkage task is one of sorting individuals according to surname and date of vital event and attempting to eliminate non-family members who happen to have the same name. Here the role of the surname portion of the individual proper names could be said to be that of a sorting item, pure and simple. In the case of parish records which record the names of both parents at marriages and births, the continuity of double surnames is a highly identificatory feature, though mis-spellings, deaths and remarriages may complicate things a little.

In the second kind of record linkage, personal record linkage, a certain amount of pre-linkage of the records occurs as well. Census rolls, for example, are already specimens of family reconstitution of a limited sort. Marriage records, club memberships, newspaper items are loosely linked according to date. However, in cases of personal record linkage we may wish to collect a group of records which all pertain to a particular individual. Under what conditions is such a grouping of records possible? The answer is clearly: whenever the records in question contain sufficient identifying information in common to enable us to ascribe them severally to the same individual. In practice, the items which are common to A and B are not necessarily common to B and C. But the linkage relation L is a transitive relation in that we hold that if A is linked to B and B to C then we hold that A is linked to C even if A and C contain an insufficient number of identifying items in common. It is an interesting logical point that in record linkage practice we do not necessarily require that in such cases A and C have a sufficient number of identifying items in common. But would we be willing to consider A and C linked if they contained no identifying items in common?

We might at this point ask ourselves what an ideal identifying item would be like. It seems clear that such an item would be of a sort which was present on all records which are potentially linkable, just as a painter puts his unique sign or signature on each of his paintings. In practice, of course, this does not happen. We believe that all of Winston Churchill's records are his not because they all have a unique identifying item present but because we found the records in his house or his safe or in his wife's keeping. Or, perhaps, because they were all in his hand or his secretary's and so on. Still an ideal identifying item would be one which was present on all records of a potentially linkable sort. Further, it should be highly individual, unique. For if an identifying item could also be used by another individual (or family of individuals) then confusion might result . . . as it often does when we have 500 J. Smiths in a file pair. Finally, an ideal identifying item would have no tendency to be mis-spelled or in error from record to record. In record linkage practice many devices are employed to circumvent problems of mis-spelling or mis-recording identifying items, particularly in names, but ideally the problem would not arise.

So the three ideal features for an identifying item are: universal presence, uniqueness and freedom from error. Identifying items can be ranked according to the degrees of these features which they possess. On any such ranking, ordinary proper names come out rather well. In fact it might be suspected that the institution of human proper names exists mainly because there is no natural feature of human beings which fulfills these requirements. This gives the social historian a quite different account of the proper name from the philosopher. For the social historian a proper name is a good all round identifying item in that it is almost universally present on records of his interest, largely unique (although not absolutely so) and relatively error free. Sometimes, of course, there exist variations of surname spellings: Shakspear, Shakespear, Shakespeare, Shakspere, etc. But often no confusion results since they all sound alike. In the case of Englishmen on a path of social elevation due to the death of a relative or the whim of a king or prime minister, the name changes are easily followed and often two names are given: Edward de Vere, Earl of Oxford; Disraeli, Earl of Beaconsfield.

The social historian's account of a proper name, far from suggesting that it is backed by mysterious descriptive phrases which the historian would really like to assert, suggests that proper names are indispensable in social history so that we can link records at all. And without record linkage history would be a mass of isolated facts. Any historian who eliminated proper names from his records and used only the descriptive items on the record in question instead would find the record linkage task impossible to accomplish, or nearly so.

HISTORICAL INDIVIDUATION AND PREDICATION

At this point a philosopher might turn on us. For, he might say, you have ignored the crucial questions. Your account is only an account of the function of proper names in social history. But what we want to know is what a social historian is entitled to assert. He may need the proper names for record linkage purposes, but once he has used them for that purpose, has he any right to use such names thereafter to refer to the person who has generated his linked pairs or groups of records? Oughtn't he then to take the more modest course and delete the proper names and refer only to the person by means of descriptive phrases?

It seems to me that a parallel might be drawn here between historical individuation by means of record linkage and the identification of dreams by means of tales told the next morning. Some philosophers wrongly suggest that we do not really have dreams. The only reality is the story we tell the next morning about events which purportedly went on while we slept. Now there is an interesting parallel here. We believe what people tell us about their dreams because there is no possible way we could question them. Similarly, when we assemble pairs or groups of linked records under the same identifying item set, there is no sense in asking whether or not those identifying items or that name really were the identifying items and name of the person we are identifying. We just cannot go any deeper than we have gone. It seems to me further that this should not lead us to doubt our procedure any more than we should wonder, when we relate a dream in the morning, whether it really was a dream we had or is merely a story we are making up on the spur of the moment; not a real memory but a mere supposed memory.

In other words, philosophical discussion here does touch a real ground. The ground is that historical assertions are controlled by record linkage. Historical assertion which makes no appeal to record linkage—and I do not mean simply to records—is uncontrolled speculation. It is as if we were to speculate about another man's dreams without asking him what he dreamt. Or it is as if we announced a mathematical proposition and expected everybody to believe it and yet offered no proof. Or it is as if we announced a physical law but could show no experiments or observations to back it up.

What is peculiar about the ground of history, like other grounds, is that deeper than that one cannot go. A historian might question this or that case of record linkage and have good reason too. He might think that Hengist existed but Horsa did not. But he could not, without insanity, seriously doubt all record linkages any more than a mathematician could suddenly wake up doubting all proofs. For this would amount, in both cases, to doubting the fundamental procedures of their art. If the historian asks for assurance that record linkage procedures are in general valid, what he is asking for is a proof of the certainty of an algorithm. But algorithms cannot be proved. Proofs presuppose algorithms.

This gives us a definition of history which I hope will be quite uncontroversial, namely, that history is speculation about the past which is controlled by record linkage (and often by nominal record linkage).

David Herlihy

2 Problems of record linkages in Tuscan fiscal records of the fifteenth century

The investigator who seeks, whether by manual or by automatic means, to link historical records will often encounter two principal problems. He must initially determine whether a person, family, object or event mentioned in one document can be found also in another.[1] Even if satisfactory identifications can be made, he may then face another, more subtle, but no less formidable difficulty. In many and perhaps most instances, the investigator will be interested not primarily in the persons he successfully traces but in the entire population of which, he hopes, they will be a representative sample. But the process of tracing persons will almost always involve a process of selection; simply put, in almost every society, some persons are more stable and more visible than others. This then raises the second problem: do the persons who have left the deepest tracks in the historical record constitute a true random sample of their statistical universe, on the basis of which reliable inferences can be made concerning the entire population? The investigator must consider the chance that record linkages, the very successes of his research, have introduced biases into his data. If biases become apparent, and if his documents permit, perhaps he can in his calculations compensate for them. At least he must determine where in his conclusions he should be cautious.

In this chapter we shall consider both problems of identification and bias in regard to a particular fund of documents—Tuscan fiscal records of the fifteenth century. Over the past five years an international team of scholars has prepared a partial, machine-readable

---

[1] For simplicity we shall pretend in the following discussion that we are interested only in tracing persons and families. The situation would not, however, be substantially different if we were concerned with an object, such as a piece of property listed in several tax rolls, or an event, to which several sources refer.

edition of a principal part of this documentary deposit—the Catasto of 1427—but are only now entering the phase of the research in which record linkages assume a major importance.[2] While we have as yet conceived no grand strategy, we have perceived several difficulties which obstruct the tracing of individuals or distort the results to be expected even when they are found. We hope that our experiences may contribute to the broad fund of information, of which historians have need, if they are to realize the enormous promise which modern capabilities of data processing now create.

In reviewing our own experiences, some few words are needed to describe the character of Tuscan fiscal records of the fifteenth century.[3] In 1427, in the face of a mounting financial crisis, the commune of Florence reformed its system of direct taxation in the interest of both greater fairness and efficiency. The reform of 1427 took on an almost mythical quality for Florentines of subsequent generations, who remembered it as a triumph of justice and the very salvation of the city's independence in the face of its foreign enemies.[4] The new tax system was grounded upon a comprehensive effort to identify who in the Florentine state could pay taxes, and how much. The determination of ability to pay required a detailed survey, called a Catasto, which included in its purview the entire Florentine domain. In 1427, within the province of Tuscany, only the cities and terri-

---

[2] The work in Europe has been carried on under the direction of Mme. Christiane Klapisch of the Centre de Recherches Historiques of the Ecole des Hautes Etudes. The project has been supported by the Centre National de Recherche Scientifique in France and the National Science Foundation in America. Brief descriptions of the project may be found in Christiane Klapisch, 'Fiscalité et démographie en Toscane (1427–1430)', *Annales-Economies, Sociétés, Civilisations*, XXIV (1969), 1313–37; David Herlihy, 'Vieillir au Quattrocento', *Annales*, XXIV (1969), 1338–52; *idem*, 'The Tuscan town in the Quattrocento—a demographic profile', *Medievalia et Humanistica*, new series, I (1970), 81–109.

[3] On the character of these records, see especially Elio Conti, *I catasti agrari della Repubblica fiorentina e il catasto particellare toscano secoli XIV–XIX* (Rome: Istituto Storico Italiano per il Medio Evo, 1966). The regulations creating the Catasto have been edited by O. Karmin, *La legge del catasto fiorentino del 1427* (Florence, 1906).

[4] In 1458, when the Catasto was reinstituted in the city, the prologue to the enabling legislation referred to the reform of 1427 as 'the defense and the salvation of liberty'—'la difensione e salute della libertà'. See Reg. 2, 79v, copy of law dated 10 January 1458. (In this article, registers cited without further specifications refer to the volumes in the Catasto deposit at the Archivio di Stato of Florence; the dates of the documents are adjusted to the modern calendar.) According to the prologue, the previous fiscal system had generated strife among the people, ruined widows and orphans, and forced many citizens to wander as beggars through the world. For the expression of a similar sentiment, see Niccolo Machiavelli, Istorie fiorentine, IV, 14, *Opere*, ed. Ezio Raimondi (Milan, 1969), p. 505, who says that the reform of 1427 was accomplished over the protests of the *potenti*, the wealthy and the powerful. The wealthy particularly objected to the inclusion of liquid assets in the tax base, upon which Florentine commerce and the city's prosperity were, in their opinion, critically dependent.

tories of Lucca and Siena were independent of Florentine rule. The
Florentine subjects settled in this fairly extensive geographic area
included nearly 60,000 households and slightly more than 260,000
persons. With an astounding confidence in its administrative resources, the Florentine commune undertook to survey all these
households, both their properties and their members. According to
the enabling legislation of May 1427, each household head in
Florence, its countryside and its subject territories was required to
present a description of his assets and liabilities. Assets included real
estate (each field had to be recorded with its location, size and
harvests), merchandise, animals, cash, accounts receivable, and
shares in the public debt. Outstanding debts and the rent paid for the
family dwelling were reckoned as liabilities. The household head was
further required to name and describe everyone resident in his household—his or her sex, age, relationship to the head, skills and even
health. These preliminary declarations drawn up by the household
heads and deposited with the tax officials were called Portate.

Once received by the tax officials, the Portate were reviewed and
checked for accuracy and honesty, and then they were completely
recopied in clean draft. These fair copies of the declarations, preserved in large volumes, are called the Campioni, and they represent
the official version of the survey. The officials proceeded to calculate
and enter into the Campioni a figure which represented the taxpayer's assets less his liabilities, that is, his ability to pay. The tax
officials also imposed a head tax on all able-bodied adult males
between 18 and 60 years of age in the city and between 14 and 70 in
the countryside. They allowed residents of the city of Florence to
deduct from their taxable assets 200 florins per household member;
residents of the city of Pisa could deduct 50 florins per member. In
other words, the method of calculating the tax differed among
Florence, Pisa and the countryside, but everywhere the information
upon which the calculations were based was the same. Finally, on the
basis of the Campioni, special summaries (Sommari) were redacted,
which carried the most relevant information concerning each household—name of the household head, taxable wealth, number of adult
males subject to the head tax, and (sometimes) total size of the
household.

The redaction of the Catasto of 1427 in its three separate versions
demanded an enormous effort and expense, greater even than the
Florentine commune seems to have anticipated. The initial schedules
were rarely met, and the expenses of collecting, recording and processing the data soared. The cost of the survey in the first year alone

reportedly ran up to 5,000 florins, and the tax office at its busiest periods employed a small army of more than 70 full-time scribes.[5] The sixteen volumes of Campioni containing the declarations of the city were officially deposited in the communal treasury (*incamerati*, as the act was called) on 30 June 1428, after which further changes were to be allowed in them only under unusual circumstances. The 31 volumes of Campioni from the Florentine countryside and the ten from Pisa were finished in June 1429, and the rest of the survey completed in 1430.[6] The bulk of these records has survived, constituting an enormous mass of statistical documentation which over the years has evoked the respect and wonder of scholars.[7]

The Florentine commune intended to conduct similar surveys in the city every three years, and in the countryside every five. As the legislation of 1427 required, a new urban survey was made in 1430 and again in 1433, but deterioration in the comprehensiveness and quality of the documents became at once apparent.[8] This deteriora-

[5] Reg. 1, 57v, 3 February 1458, 'che si ragiona che le spese del primo anno del primo catasto montarono fiorini 5000 in più . . .' Although this estimate of costs is late, it seems to be accurate. On 30 June 1427, the estimated cost simply of recopying the Catasto volumes was 2000 florins, and the time required not less than six months. Cf. Reg. 2, 26r. The lists of expenses incurred by the tax officials are given in detail in Reg. 4 and ff. The busiest time for the tax office seems to have been in the early months of 1429, when the scribes were occupied in copying the lengthy rural Catasti. For example, on 3 May 1429, 79 notaries and 2 servants were hired for two months (Reg. 6, 7v); each scribe received the handsome salary of 5 florins per month. With such high salaries, and with further costs for supplies, the estimate of 5000 florins as the cost of taking the survey seems reasonable for the first year, and probably also for the two following years as well.

[6] See Reg. 1, 26r, 30 June 1429, for a list of the state of the various versions of the survey as of that date. The sixteen volumes of Campioni of the city of Florence, 31 volumes from the countryside, and ten volumes from Pisa were by then all complete. Moreover, 'scripte et registra', that is, the Portate or preliminary declarations had been collected from the inhabitants of the subject territories, religious and ecclesiastics, the guilds, and the foreigners. The only regions which had not yet made the declarations were the city and county of Volterra and the Florentine possessions in the Romagna. In the latter region, because of a recent Milanese invasion, it was considered unwise to force the inhabitants to make declarations, lest their loyalty to Florence be undermined.

[7] Two of the 31 original volumes of Campioni from the countryside of Florence have not survived, but it is possible to reconstruct their content in large part through the information contained in the Portate and the Sommari. There are similar gaps in the series of Portate, but here too most of the information they contained can be found in the two other versions of the survey. In spite of sporadic losses, the state of preservation of this huge documentary fund is excellent.

[8] The second Catasto of the city was 'incamerato' on 30 June 1431, but because of the many omissions and errors which at once became noticeable, additions and changes had to be allowed by a special law enacted in July. Cf. Reg. 7, 32r, 23 August 1431, where 30 persons were added; on 27 August, 26 more declarations were added. In the following year (Reg. 9, 8r, 15 July 1432) it was noted that 'proxime preteriti officiales fecerunt plures additiones pluribus hominibus et postas catastorum.' Evidently the tax officials had encountered considerable difficulty finding all the household heads and reporting their possessions accurately.

tion had at least the fortunate result of preserving the value of the first survey of 1427, which continued to be consulted on tax matters through the fifteenth century and even beyond; doubtless, this continuing utility of the Catasto of 1427 is the principal reason for its survival.

After 1433, Florence did not attempt to make another survey of its own city until 1458–9, when again fiscal pressures forced it to seek new funds 'by way of the Catasto', as the enabling legislation describes it.[9] The Catasto was renewed in 1469–70 and again in 1480.[10] In the countryside, the commune undertook surveys in 1435–7, 1444–7 and 1451–5, but these have been preserved in so confused a state as to be virtually unusable. With the restoration of the Catasto in the city, efforts were again made to take similar surveys in the countryside; Estimi or Catasti dating from 1458–60, 1469–71, 1480 and 1487 have survived. Florence never seems to have included the subject cities in these surveys as it had in 1427. In the later urban surveys, the commune abandoned all effort to determine precisely the value of a taxpayer's liquid assets. We are told that the constant inspection of the ledgers of Florentine merchants prompted many of them to keep several sets of books, some for the benefit of the tax inspectors and the others to record the true state of the business.[11] In an effort to make the tax system fair and remunerative, but less expensive to administer, the commune introduced a tax 'by way of scale', that is, graduated according to the taxpayer's wealth. According to the final scale, established in 1481, the poorest taxpayers, with property of 50 florins or less, had to pay 7 per cent per year of their assessment figure, while the richest with more than 400 florins paid 22 per cent.[12] But these ingenious efforts could not compensate for the growing chaos in the tax administration, and did not still the protests, particularly on the part of the merchants, that high tax levels were ruining the commerce upon which Florence's prosperity depended.

In response to such pleas Florence in 1495 abandoned a system of direct tax 'by way of the Catasto', in favour of a new, much simpler system, 'by way of the tithe'. This was called the Decima, or Tithe,

[9] Reg. 2, 79v, for the enabling legislation.   [10] Reg. 2, 101r and ff.

[11] Reg. 2, 89v, 22 August 1458. '. . . volgarmente si dice chiaschuno merchatante essersi acconcio in fare più libri . . .' The careful scrutiny of the mercantile accounts was allegedly driving capital from the city, to the grave injury of Florentine commerce. To alleviate this difficulty, the tax officials and the household heads were henceforth simply to agree on a fair figure representing their liquid assets, without detailed inspection of the books.

[12] Reg. 2, 128r, 8 November 1481.

of the Republic.[13] It was to be based on an assessment of real property only, with no consideration taken of the demographic characteristics of the household. Every year, a tax equal to 10 per cent of the value of the household's possessions in real property was to be paid. The volumes of the Decima have also survived, but are far less revealing than the older Catasto surveys, and incomparable with the first Catasto of 1427. As one historian has remarked, the abandonment of the Catasto closes an extraordinary window, looking out over Tuscan life and society in the fifteenth century.[14]

In seeking to gather and control data on the demographic characteristics and the wealth of its population, the Florentine commune made use of one tactic which is of especial interest to historians. The Catasto officials sought systematically to link their own records, in the sense of comparing the information coming from various sources concerning the same taxpayer. Before 1427, the principal means by which the commune collected money from its subjects was the forced loan or Prestanza in the city, and the Estimo, or proportionate direct tax, in the countryside. Of the rural Estimi, the most recent had been redacted between October 1422 and August 1426; it was finished, in other words, less than a year before the Catasto was introduced. The records of those required to extend loans or pay rural taxes provided the officials with a list of names and an approximate estimate of wealth which were carefully compared with the results of the Catasto survey.[15] Moreover, the three versions of the Catasto were also closely linked. The scribes who copied the Portate into the volumes of Campioni carefully noted the page where the official version could be found. So also, the summary volumes carry references to the location of the full declarations. The Catasto officials—and the historian—could and can move with considerable ease from one version to another.

Further, in spite of the deterioration of the Catasto after 1427, the

[13] See the copy of the enabling legislation, dated 3 February 1495, in Reg. 2, 129r, which refers to an earlier law passed in December 1494, requiring that the new tax distribution 'si dovesse fare in su beni immobili per non alterare gli exercitii et traffichi della nostra città de' quali tanto fiorito e si grande popolo per la maggiore parte si pasce et nutricha . . .'

[14] Referring specifically to the rural Catasti, Elio Conti has remarked (Catasti agrari, p. 117), 'Ma con la fine delle denunce fiscali, di fronte a noi si chiude una straordinaria finestra sul mondo contadino.'

[15] According to the Catasto regulations (Reg. 1, 2v, 24 May 1427), the new survey was to include every 'florentinum civem seu alium qui in civitate Florentie deberet prestantias vel alia quecumque similia honera.' The rural Catasti included everyone 'descriptum vel comprehensum in ultima distributione extimi ordinarii comitatus incameratum de mense agusti proximi preterito . . . nullo excluso . . .' The amount of the *prestanza* or *estimo* borne by each household head was also entered upon his Catasto declaration.

commune attempted to check the results of later surveys against the initial survey of 1427. For example, in redacting the third urban Catasto of 1433, the officials ordered that the two previous surveys be reviewed and that names found there but not included in the redaction of 1433 were to be added to it; only the dead were to be excused.[16] In the later surveys of 1458-9 and 1469-70 the declarations carry references telling where the householder, his ancestor, and the properties he held appeared in the Catasto of 1427. An effort was similarly made to trace sales and donations of property, to make sure that such transfers did not allow the property to slip unnoticed from the tax rolls. Through observing the successes and the failures of contemporary efforts to trace individuals, the historian can determine what segments of society were likely to elude the most rigorous scrutiny. We shall return to this important point.

In spite of Florence's inability to maintain the Catasto at its original levels of quality and comprehensiveness, this magnificent document still offers almost endless possibilities of investigating Florentine society in the fifteenth century. Moreover, the Florentine archives have preserved an abundance of other records, which invite comparison and linkages with the Catasto. We have, for example, lists of Florentine citizens which give their years of birth, and which offer the opportunity to check rather well the accuracy of age reporting in the Catasto.[17] The survival of this huge survey, and the possibility of tying it with other records, promise a range of information which probably could not be equalled in regard to any other contemporary society.

To trace individuals through or across such sets of records primarily requires a comparison of nominal lists. To do this well, the historian must first learn how individuals received their names, how they used them, and how they were reported. In our work difficulties have appeared in all three areas. In the fifteenth century, the use of family names in Tuscan society remained largely confined to the richer classes of the city; the poorer and the rural families must be traced through constantly shifting Christian names and patronyms. Moreover, for all classes a principal source of confusion in comparing nominal lists is the preference which families retained for certain names, so much so that they gave the same names to more than a single child. Family memoirs, called Ricordi or Ricordanze, give a

---

[16] Reg. 1, 58r, 7 September 1434.

[17] Archivio di Stato di Firenze, Tratte, Reg. 39, 'Hic est liber sive quaternus continens in se declarationes etatum civium florentinorum civitatis Florentie cum ipsorum nominibus prenominibus anno mense et die originis ipsorum. . . .' The list was originally redacted in 1429, but additions were made up to 1456.

good insight into the naming practices of the Florentines. If a child died, the family frequently bestowed the name of the deceased child upon the next born of the same sex. The memoirs of the Corsini family (the bishop of Florence was a Corsini in 1427) give several examples of this. Matteo di Niccolò Corsini named no less than three of his sons Bartolomeo, born in 1378, 1379, and 1389 respectively; two were named Ludovico, two Giovanni; and three girls were called Giovanna.[18] Giovanni di Matteo Corsini, who appears in the Catasto, named a girl born in 1427 Lisabetta; after her death in 1428, he named another girl, born in 1430, also Lisabetta.[19] Matteo di Giovanni Corsini called one son, born in 1435, Giovanni, and after his death in 1441, gave the same name to another son born in 1443; he called two girls Gostanza, born in 1441 and 1446 respectively.[20] As recorded in the memoirs, the middle names of these children usually differed, but unfortunately, in most nominal lists, including those preserved in the Catasto, middle names are not recorded. Typically, to judge again from the memoirs, the name was not used again until the death of a previous bearer, but there seem to have been exceptions. Matteo Corsini named a second son Bartolomeo while a first Bartolomeo was still living (he died a year later). Perhaps the ill health of the older child prompted the father to take this precaution. One is reminded of the statement of the historian Edward Gibbon (1737–94), who reported that his younger brothers (he had four) were also baptized Edward, because his own ill health convinced his father that he would not survive childhood.[21] The strong preference for certain names, and the practice of bestowing

[18] *Il Libro di ricordanze dei Corsini (1362–1457)*, ed. Armando Pertrucci (Fonti per la Storia d'Italia, 100; Rome, 1965), pp. 89–95. The first Bartolomeo, Bartolomeo Bernardo, survived from 31 March 1378, to March 1379; Bartolomeo Giovanni lived from 22 June 1379, to 22 November 1390; Bartolomeo Agostino was born 26 August 1389, and died right after baptism. A Ludovico was born 22 August 1363, and died in September of the same year; Ludovico Niccolaio was born on 31 August 1374, and there seems to be no record of his death. A Giovanni Simone was born on 30 October 1376, and no mention is made of his death; another Giovanni was born on 25 May 1388, and 'died at once'. A Giovanna was born on 12 July 1369, and died the same day; another Giovanna was born on 22 February 1382, and died 'on the present day'; the third Giovanna was born on an unstated day in 1387 and 'died at once'.

[19] *Il Libro di ricordanze*, p. 139. The first was called Lisabetta e Margherita, and the second Lisabetta e Lodovica.

[20] *Il Libro di ricordanze*, pp. 143–5. The first boy was called Giovanni e Salvadore and the second Giovanni e Bernardo. The first Gostanza was Gostanza e Alessandra and the second Gostanza e Agata.

[21] 'So feeble was my constitution, so precarious my life, that in the baptism of each of my brothers, my father's prudence repeated my Christian name of Edward, that in case of the departure of the eldest son, this patronymic appellation might be still perpetuated in the family.' Edward Gibbon, *Memoirs of my life*, ed. Georges A. Bonnard (London, 1966), p. 28.

them on more than a single child, seems to have been a widespread custom in traditional European societies.

When we have explicit sources such as family memoirs, such duplications can be satisfactorily noticed and controlled. But when we have only nominal lists, it is clearly very difficult to be certain that a person, especially a child, mentioned in one source is really the same as a person in another, even though he bears an identical name. For this reason we have not attempted to estimate such demographic characteristics of the population as the survival of children, through comparing nominal lists preserved in the Catasto series.

The use of names in the fifteenth century in Tuscany presents a further set of problems. Then as now, the Italians loved to shorten or enlarge names, and their language permitted them a great and colourful range of forms for the same basic name. Nanni for Giovanni, Menico for Domenico, Vestro for Silvestro, Teo for Matteo, Cola for Niccola, Maso for Tommaso, Papi for Iacopo, Cecco for Francesco—this is only a partial list of the most common and the most evident name abbreviations. Suffixes too were favoured—Masaccio for Maso, Donatello for Donato, Giovannello for Giovanni, Marchetto for Marco, and so forth. The use of nicknames, bearing no philological connection with the Christian names, is also common, and even more difficult to control. The form of a person's name not only could vary from document to document, but also could shift in the course of the same record.[22] And it goes without saying that all names show endless variations in spelling in the fifteenth century.

Finally, in laboriously copying these records, the scribes themselves were responsible for numerous errors. Given the volume of the tedious work they accomplished, this is hardly surprising. The tax officials had to hear frequent complaints concerning such *errores calami, errori di penna*. In August 1429, for example, the officials heard a report concerning sixteen common errors in the rural Catasti. The sixth error stated 'that for [some taxpayers] there are mistakes in the name. Antonio is read instead of Attaviano, and so forth'.[23] In response, the officials could only order that the errors should be corrected when discovered, even though the Campioni volumes were

---

[22] Occasionally, the same household head was entered into the Campioni twice, under two different forms of his name. Cf. Reg. 307, 603, declaration of Papi di Stefano and 616, declaration of Iacopo di Stefano. Only after the declarations were transcribed into the Campioni did it emerge that these were the same man. Such duplicate declarations are encountered fairly often.

[23] Reg. 1, 31r, 2 August 1429. 'D'alchuni altri sono errati i nomi. Dice Antonio vuol dire Attaviano o simili errori.'

supposed to be closed to further changes. But undoubtedly, many mistakes slipped through.

Fluctuations and errors in names required that we adopt a special strategy in preparing the Catasto for computer analysis. In most respects, we considered that our work was analogous to the preparation of printed editions, to be governed by the conventional rules for the editing of manuscripts.[24] But we also recognized that the matching of names is one of the valuable services which the computer can efficiently perform, and that this would be rendered decidedly more complex if the computer had to face the original, perpetually changing orthography. We therefore decided to standardize name spellings and to enter them in most instances as they would be spelled in modern Italian, which is to say, phonetically. In other words, Iachopo, Iacoppo, and Iaccopo were all entered as Iacopo. As we now review the printouts of our edition, it is apparent that we and those who helped in the coding were not entirely successful in achieving this ideal of standardized spellings. Pagolo or Paolo, Geri or Gieri, Chino or Cino are such variants still occasionally found. But we have at least reduced greatly the range of variations, and it would represent a fairly easy task to ask the computer to complete the work of standardization, to convert every Pagolo to Paolo, or vice versa. In coding, we did not, however, attempt to resolve shortened forms into their full spellings, as for example, Teo into Matteo, Papi into Iacopo, or Meo into Bartolomeo, and so forth. The ambiguities seemed to be too many, but this too might be attempted. Whether we or others will attempt such resolutions will largely depend on how successful linkages can be when the original forms of the names are respected. We are still seeking the most efficient strategy. As for errors in the names, as well as in other parts of the declarations, we could do no more than compare the three versions of the Catasto in order to determine the best reading. Usually, we took the reading of the Campioni, as this was the version subject to the most careful scrutiny and the most extensive corrections on the part of the tax officials.

In matching records with the Catasto declarations, our strategy has so far been simple but fairly effective. The computer is asked to re-arrange the declarations of an urban precinct or a rural village in alphabetical order, and this is compared with the document to which links are sought. Affirmative or negative conclusions concerning the

---

[24] In our partial edition, we are, however, carrying the name only of the household head and not of all members of his household. This makes identifications difficult, but in doubtful cases it is usually possible to seek confirmation through returning to the original document.

identification of persons rest not on names alone, but on comparing the range of information which the two sets of records may provide—age, occupation, residence, wealth, and the like. Our basis of decision regarding the identifications of persons thus depends on what information is provided and ultimately on what type of document is being compared with the Catasto. Identification will be rejected if

1   the Christian names, patronymics and family names are not identical or common variants of the same names
2   ages do not correspond at least within ten years, to allow for the possibility of age rounding
3   information on wealth, when given, places the persons in different social categories
4   they reside in separate and distant neighbourhoods, unless there is explicit reference to immigration or emigration.

Given the variety and frequent complexity of the information to be compared, the computerization of this process has not so far appeared feasible. Because of our mass of data, we tend to exclude rather rigorously matchings which do not satisfy the above criteria; even with these losses, our documentation remains substantial. In linking records, the computer therefore performs for us only the task of re-arranging nominal lists in alphabetical order. It is a simple service, but the work would be much harder, longer and less accurate without its help.

Comparisons of nominal lists have given us an insight into the second major problem of record linkages—the biases which even successful matchings are likely to generate. The biases stem from two principal sources. First, the character and comprehensiveness of the sources could vary over time, even when superficially or officially remaining the same. The later Catasti, for example, were supposed to include the entire community, but it is clear that they did not. In 1458–9, the survey in the city counted only 7,682 households, a marked decline from the 9,780 households recorded in 1427, not including the additions made in 1428–9 and 1429–30.[25] To judge from other sources, Florence had not fallen by 21 per cent in population between the two surveys.[26] The Catasto of 1458–9 seems to have been

[25] Cf. the Sommario volumes, Reg. 834–37, and the declarations, Reg. 785 and ff. In the later surveys, the commune abandoned the practice of recopying the declarations as Campioni, but insisted that the taxpayer provide two identical copies of his declarations, upon which the calculations establishing his assessment were entered directly.

[26] J. Beloch, *Bevölkerungsgeschichte Italiens*, II (Berlin, 1940), p. 137, estimates that the taxable population of Florence was 38,765 in 1458; 41,250 in 1469, and 39,990 in 1480. As it had been 38,000 in 1427, the population shows an evident stability over the middle decades of the fifteenth century.

considerably less inclusive of the urban households. We can also discern with some certainty where the omissions were concentrated. In 1427, 3,081 households, or 31 per cent, had no taxable fortune after deductions were taken. In keeping with the rigour of the first Catasto survey, the status of these persons was carefully inspected and a separate nominal list of those without assets, the *miserabili*, was prepared.[27] In 1458–9, only 13 per cent of the households appear with no assessment.[28] The tax administration was no longer bothering to include in its survey all those who could not pay.

The declining comprehensiveness of the Catasto, even in the city where the administration functioned most efficiently, poses grave problems for its use as a historical source. It would be possible to trace many households from 1427 to 1458—the cross references are there—but given the neglect of the poor in the later surveys, the successes would inevitably include a disproportionate number of the wealthy. The sample generated by linking the series of Catasti would not, in other words, be truly representative of the experiences of the entire population.

Distortions generated by record linkages are, however, not exclusively to be attributed to the changing policies of those to whom we owe these documents. They are also rooted in a fundamental characteristic of medieval society—perhaps we should have written traditional society. That characteristic is the pronounced mobility of the population, which did not however affect all social strata equally.

We can illustrate that mobility, and the problems it creates for linking records, by turning our attention to one part of the Catasto archives. Even before the Catasto was redacted, apparently from 1372, the Florentine commune developed the practice of basing new surveys upon the old, in order to assure that a minimum of household heads escaped inclusion.[29] In redacting a new rural tax or Estimo, for example, the officials compared the resident population with the households described in the previous registration. Those who appeared in the previous survey were called the *stanti*, the ones who had stayed or remained in the village; those new to the village, not included in previous surveys, were the *tornati* or *venuti*—the newcomers; those in the older survey who had left the village were the

[27] Lists of those declared 'miserabili' are contained for two precincts (*gonfaloni*) of the city in Reg. 3, 25v and ff.

[28] Out of a sample of 743 households, 109 carried no assessment.

[29] Cf. Conti, *Catasti rurali*, p. 15, for the efforts made, apparently from 1372 to control the movements of the population in order to increase the number of households included in the newer surveys.

usciti. The dead were also noted. The list was in addition checked by the local administrators, the rural *podestà*, who governed districts in the countryside. If they knew of a man not included in the Estimo, they would have him added under the category of *trovati*, 'those found'.

In the Catasto archives at Florence, there are two volumes, each including a quarter of the countryside (Santo Spirito and San Giovanni respectively) which classify the rural heads of households in the above categories—residents, immigrants, emigrants, and those found by the administrative officials.[30] Unfortunately, we have not so far found the two volumes encompassing the two remaining quarters, which would give us a comprehensive view of movements in the countryside. The survey seems to have been completed before July 1425, and was probably taken not in preparation for the Catasto itself, but for the rural Estimo which was finished in August 1426.[31] Still, the light it casts on population movements in the villages must have interested the redactors of the Catasto as well, and probably for this reason the two volumes have been preserved as part of the Catasto archives.

This survey of those remaining in, arriving at and departing from the villages invites comparison with the Catasto, redacted approximately two years later. Such a comparison can help answer three important questions:

1   how mobile was the population in the rural villages?
2   is mobility associated with wealth or social status?
3   do the more stable members of the community have perceptibly different demographic characteristics from those who are mobile?

To answer these questions, we have taken as a sample the rural district (*pieve*) of Santa Maria Impruneta, some six miles south of Florence in the direction of the Chianti hills.[32] It included in 1427

---

[30] Reg. 106 (Q. di Santo Spirito) and 166 (Q. di San Giovanni).

[31] Reg. 106, 7v, where an entry is cancelled, and the cancellation bears the date 4 July 1425; another cancellation on the same folio is dated 8 July 1425. These dates are therefore a *terminus ante quem* for the redaction of this volume of the survey. The comparison of those individuals for whom ages are given (if we exclude those instances when rounding is apparent, e.g. when the person is age 70 in both surveys, or has increased in age by exactly five years) shows that the ages differ from one to three years, with two being the most common difference.

[32] The declarations are in Reg. 307. On Impruneta, see my article 'Santa Maria Impruneta: a rural commune in the late Middle Ages', *Florentine Studies. Politics and society in Renaissance Florence*, ed. Nicolai Rubinstein (London, 1968), pp. 242–76.

Table 1 Mobility of the population at Impruneta, c. 1425–7

	Residents (Stanti)	Immigrants (Tornati)	Emigrants (Usciti)	Added (Trovati)	Not found	Total
Households	209	99	2	1	65	376
Per cent	55·6	26·3	0·5	0·2	17·4	
Persons	1,271	466	9	8	304	2,058
Per cent	61·8	22·6	0·4	0·4	14·8	
Average household size	6·08	4·71	4·50	8·00	4·68	5·47
No. children (age 0–15)	512	165	5	2	119	803
Average no. per household	2·45	1·67	2·50	2·00	1·83	2·14
Average age population	29·38	31·10	23·50	40·25	28·39	29·64
Average wealth (florins)	78·88	26·40	97·50	8·00	19·08	54·63

Source: ASF. Catasto, Reg. 307 and Reg. 106. 'Households' are those contained in the Catasto survey of 1427. The classifications are based on the earlier survey of c. 1425.

eighteen villages, 376 households, and 2,058 persons. To make our comparisons, we have worked backwards from the Catasto to determine how many household heads, or a parent or relative, were to be found in the survey taken some two years previously, how they were classified, and what were the chief economic and demographic characteristics of the separate categories.

The results of these comparisons, presented in Table 1, show that only about 83 per cent of the household heads listed in the Catasto were known in the villages of Impruneta in the earlier survey, or had an ancestor recorded in it. For all practical purposes, the 17 per cent of household heads previously unrecorded represent further additions to the group of *tornati*, that is, new arrivals in the villages. Only between 50 and 60 per cent of the household heads in 1427 (or their parents) were classified as *stanti*, established residents, in the earlier survey. Probably, conditions peculiar to Impruneta contributed to a high level of mobility; the distinct was close to the city, and it included many farms held under short-term leases (the *mezzadria*). On the other hand, from a superficial consideration of the entries for other villages in other regions of the countryside, the levels of mobility seem to have been surprisingly high; roughly a quarter of the household heads seem to have been recent arrivals, *tornati*. But this will be more accurately measured in subsequent analyses.

Most notable for our purposes are the contrasts in wealth and household characteristics between the stable and mobile segments of this society—the *stanti* in comparison with the *tornati* and those who appear in the villages only in 1427. (For completeness, we have also included the *usciti* and *trovati* in the table, but clearly they are too few to allow us to draw conclusions concerning these groups.) With an average assessment before deductions of 78·88 florins, the *stanti* were substantially richer than the *tornati* (31·10 florins average wealth) and the 'not found' (19·08 florins), and also were wealthier than the average for all households (54·63 florins). Poverty clearly contributed to mobility. Poverty and mobility seem also to have affected the household structure of the new arrivals. The households of the *tornati* were smaller than those of the *stanti* (4·71 versus 6·08 persons on the average) and in particular they were supporting fewer children (1·67 per household as against 2·45). Similar contrasts clearly differentiate the newest arrivals in the villages, those 'not found' in the earlier survey, from the established residents, the *stanti*. The *tornati* (though not apparently those not previously found in the villages) were also older than the *stanti*. It may be, of course, that mobile families differed from stable households because their heads were at a different point in their developmental cycles. This may partially explain the observed differences in average size and average number of children supported. But the point remains that the *stanti*, the most stable segment of the population, cannot be considered to represent a true random sample of all households in the community.

These contrasts have importance, as the *stanti*, the most stable group in the community, had the best chance of appearing in the documents. To trace their family histories through subsequent Estimi and Catasti would be highly revealing, but we would also have to be wary of concluding that the figures drawn from their experiences are characteristic of the entire community. Moderate wealth gave them a certain stability and enabled them to adopt a certain style of life. The poor lived much differently. Their need stimulated movement, reduced the size of their households (and perhaps the fertility of their marriages) and above all rendered them less visible, or at least less consistently visible, in our sources. But they still constituted a large segment of the rural community, and we cannot allow our documents and their biases to deceive us into thinking that they were not there.

We have not yet devised any effective means of providing compensation for this bias, generated by one of the fundamental characteristics of medieval Tuscan society. But our experience indicates that in seeking to link records, the researcher should keep careful count of his failures as well as his successes. A high level of failures points to a high mobility in the community being studied, and increases the likelihood that a sample of the population based on successful linkages will give a distorted picture of the population and its experiences. The distortion is likely to grow as the chronological range of the inquiry extends. There is something quite atypical about a family able to stand firm over generations when surrounded by a moving social world. Perhaps scholars will eventually be able to develop some sort of confidence table, against which scores of successful and unsuccessful linkages could be compared and from which they might draw some indication of the quality of their samples. But perhaps the more immediate task is to establish clearly the nature of the problems which affect the matching of records—problems rooted both in the documents we use and the societies we investigate. The light in which we view the distant past varies in intensity as it moves across society. We cannot really change that light, but we can find out why and by how much it varies, and thus perhaps correct our vision.

Yves Blayo

3 Name variations in a village in Brie, 1750–1860

In family reconstitution studies of populations in the past, linkage decisions are based primarily on forenames and surnames. Difficulties therefore arise because of variations in names, changes in spelling and difficulty in reading the registers. These problems are easily overcome when reconstitution is done by hand, but seem to present greater difficulty if reconstitution by computer is contemplated after a preliminary coding of forenames and surnames. The coding method must be sufficiently flexible to ensure that a surname variation does not lead to failure to link the record of an event to the family in which it occurred (which would cause the creation of a fictitious family), but equally, it must be restrictive enough to distinguish between two similar surnames, since otherwise an event will be ascribed to a family in which it did not occur. The better the solution of these two conflicting requirements, the simpler the reconstitution program and the more accurate the reconstitution itself.

I have carried out by hand a family reconstitution study of a village near Paris (Grisy-Suisnes, Seine et Marne) between 1750 and 1860. In doing so I listed all variations of each surname from the time of its first occurrence in the register. This makes it possible to assess the implications of variations in coded names for computerized reconstitution when compared with a manual reconstitution which is assumed to be completely accurate.

1   Three coding methods were examined:

   a   The Russell Soundex code soon proved unsuitable. It is ill adapted to French spelling and pronunciation and produces many fictitious families.

   b   The method used in this study consists in coding the first letter and the next two consonants, instead of the letter and three digits of the Soundex code. This method, suggested by Louis Henry, takes account of the characteristics of the French language. Thus, silent and nasalized consonants are not transcribed and double consonants or their equivalents are treated as single consonants, while diphthong vowels at the beginning of words are recorded as simple vowels, etc. Precise rules govern the various possibilities.

c   It seemed reasonable to suppose that the accentuated syllable of a surname was more stable than any other. I therefore devised a four letter code in which the last two positions were used for the consonant and vowel of the stressed syllable (in French the last syllable, or the penultimate if the last has a silent e). This method produced results very similar to those of the Henry code. I adopted the latter since it involves one less letter.

2   Since one of the main objectives of family reconstitution is the study of fertility, the effect of surname variations was measured by noting the number of births which would have been lost to the family reconstitution forms used in this study.[1]

A variation in surname on a reconstitution form was taken to be a difference between the coding of the parents' surnames on the marriage record and the coding of the surname of the father and mother on the birth record of one of the children. It follows that a childless marriage cannot produce a surname variation, and that the probability of a variation grows with the size of the family.

Only surnames were considered initially, and no link was made if there was any variation in the coding of either surname in the family. However, one might also consider forenames, and then bar linkage only if the surnames of both parents varied simultaneously, provided that the forenames did not vary. We shall examine the results of both strategies.

Manual family reconstitution of Grisy-Suisnes for the period 1750–1860 produced 445 families of types MI and MII which were in observation at least five years. Table 1 shows the frequency of at least one variation in surname by family size and date of marriage.

---

[1] These concerned the families for which the date of marriage, the date of end of observation, and the exact or approximate age at marriage of the wife, were all known, and which were in observation for at least five years (types MI and MII in the usage of French reconstitution studies).

Table 1 Grisy-Suisnes 1750–1860 : number of family reconstitution forms (type MI and MII) by date of marriage and number of children born in the village

Number of children	1750–69			1770–89			1790–1819			1820–60			Total		
	a	b	Total	a	b	Total	a	b	Total	a	b	Total	a	b	Total
0	7		7	3		3	19		19	39		39	68		68
1	4		4	1		1	19	3	22	40	3	43	64	6	70
2	2	2	4	5		5	27	2	29	45		45	79	4	83
3	5	2	7	5	3	8	20	1	21	27	2	29	57	8	65
4	4	3	7	9	1	10	12	3	15	14	3	17	39	10	49
5	4	1	5	7	1	8	13		13	7		7	31	2	33
6	2	1	3	7	1	8	5	3	8	5		5	19	5	24
7	2		2	5	1	6	7		7	6		6	20	1	21
8	4	1	5		1	1	3		3				7	2	9
9	1		1		2	2	2		2	1		1	4	2	6
10	1	1	2	1		1	3		3	1		1	6	1	7
11							1		1				1		1
12	1	1	2	2	1	3	1		1				4	2	6
13	1	1	2										1	1	2
14															
15		1	1											1	1
Total c	31	14	45	42	11	53	113	12	125	146	8	154	332	45	377
Total number of children	161	91	252	208	69	277	420	40	460	393	21	414	1182	221	1403

a   no surname variation
b   at least one surname variation
c   the first line (no child) is excluded from the totals : this produces the figures used in later tabulations

The proportion of family reconstitution forms, which at least one child, on which there was at least one variation in the coding of one of the two surnames falls steadily over time (Table 2). But this may

Table 2

	Marriages in				
	1750–69	1770–89	1790–1819	1820–60	Total
Percentage of family reconstitution forms containing at least one surname variation	31·1	20·8	9·6	5·2	11·9
Average number of children in families with at least one child	5·6	5·2	3·7	2·7	3·7
Number of births with a name variation	41	27	25	14	107
Number of these births per 100 total births	16·3	9·7	5·4	3·4	7·6

be misleading because the average number of children in families having at least one child also falls steadily cohort by cohort. Therefore, to follow the tendency towards stability and consistency in the coded spellings of names, it is necessary to establish the frequency of difference between the coded spellings of parents' names on birth records and the coded spelling of the same names on the related marriage record. The results are given on the bottom two lines in Table 2. The sharply reduced frequency of name variations in the later marriage cohorts is best appreciated in this manner.

Over the whole period 107 out of 1,403 children, or 7·6 per cent, would have been lost if surnames only had been used, without regard to forenames. On the assumption that forenames had also been coded and that they did not vary, a link would only be rejected if both surnames varied at the same time. Table 3 shows the number of re-

Table 3

	Marriages in														
	1750–69			1770–89			1790–1819			1820–60			Total		
Number of Children	a	b	c	a	b	c	a	b	c	a	b	c	a	b	c
1	5	6	1	2	2	1	4	4	1	1	4		12	16	3
2				2		1	1	1			1		3	2	1
3				2	2						1		2	3	
4		1			1						1			3	
5	1	1											1	1	
6							2						2		
7			1												1
8	1												1		
Total	7	8	2	6	5	2	7	5	1	1	7		21	25	5
		17			13			13			8			51[1]	
Number of Children	18	15	8	12	12	3	18	6	1	1	13		49	46	12
		41			27			25			14			107	

a   variation in father's surname only
b   variation in mother's surname only
c   simultaneous variation in both surnames

[1] in six out of the 45 forms with surname variations, there are several types of variation

constitution forms with at least one name variation, subdivided according to whether the variation occurred in the father's surname, the mother's surname, or both simultaneously. It also shows the number of birth records involved in each case.

The proportion of children affected by simultaneous variation in the two surnames is as follows, shown by the marriage cohort:

Marriages in:	1750–69	1770–89	1790–1819	1820–60	Total
	3·2%	1·1%	0·2%	—	0·8%

The loss of births at Grisy, for the period 1750–1860, is in total less than 1 per cent and this is certainly a lower figure than that caused by the migration of married couples. The loss was, however, substantial in the cohort of 1750–69. Marriage in this cohort produced births until almost the end of the eighteenth century. The twelve births lost in all were distributed over time as follows:

1750–59	3
1760–69	4
1770–79	1
1780–89	0
1790–99	4

They were lost because of the following surname variations:

a DELAPLAINE-LENOTTAIRE becoming LAPLAINE-NOTTAIRE
(7 cases)

b JOFFRAUX-LENORMAND „ FOFFROT-NORMAND
(1 case)

c JOUAS-CHUPIN „ JONAS-FRANCOISE
(2 cases)

d BENOIT-HAURANT „ BEZIER-MORAND
(1 case)

e MOULUT-GOGUET „ MONTUT-GODIER
(1 case)

Two thirds of the losses arose because of the suppression of the prefix DE or LE (a and b). The third name pair changed partly because of poor hand-writing (U = N in JOUAS) and partly because of the substitution of the second forename of the wife for her surname. The last instance is the combined result of handwriting (father's surname) and variable pronunciation (G = D) in the case of the mother.

The fact that surnames often changed because of the suppression of a prefix suggests that it would be wise to devise a special routine for surnames with a prefix when coding is carried out, for example by making an alphabetical list of them.

Finally, it is worth noting that in the case of five of the twelve lost births, the forenames of the parents at their marriages and on the birth records were identical. In six cases the forename of one of the parents did not change, but the forename of the other was one of the two forenames on the marriage record, or the forename at marriage preceded by Marie. In the last case, the father on the birth record has only the first, and his wife the second of the two forenames each had at marriage. The use of forenames, therefore, would reduce the loss of births to the vanishing point.

If the families at Grisy-Suisnes over the period 1750–1860 had been reconstituted by computer using the name coding methods suggested by Louis Henry, the number of births used in the study of fertility would have been underestimated by about 8 per cent if surnames alone had been used as a linkage criterion. If forenames also had been used, and had always remained stable, the loss due to simultaneous variations in the surnames of the spouses would have been less than 1 per cent over the whole period. In both cases, the maximum loss is at the beginning of the period studied. In the second case the reconstitution would have been fully satisfactory. It would be dangerous to generalize from this result however, until further studies have been made. There were three favourable circumstances in the case of Grisy-Suisnes: the handwriting of the registers set no serious problems; local pronunciation did not modify surnames as much as in some other parts of France;[2] and homonyms are infrequent chiefly because the village was small (828 inhabitants in 1806, 1,025 in 1861). The results would certainly have been less good if any of these circumstances had been different. In areas where French was not the spoken language, for example, or where a patois predominated, phonetic peculiarities, the writing down of spoken names, or indeed the translation of names were the cause of many variations.[3] Reconstitution by computer will therefore only become possible after a preliminary phonetic study of the language, dialect or patois prevalent in the area.

In closing, it is important to stress the problems which might result from the identity after coding of two pairs of surnames which were

[2] Note however: GOGUET = GODIER; CORBET = COLBET; FAREBEAU = FREREBEAU; HAVE = HERVE; JAMBON = CHAMBON; PFEIFER = FEIFER = PEIFER.

[3] For example at Germont in Deux-Sèvres: BELLANGER = BERANGER = BRANGER = BRANGIER = BRANCHE. At Saint-Paul-la-Roche in the Dordogne: ABJAT = DABJAT = DABIAT = DAIAT = DAJAT = DAJAC = DACAC = DAJAZA = DOZA; and again: BAPPART = BAPPEL = BABEL = VABER. At Boulay, in Moselle: METZGER = BOUCHER = LANIO (Latin).

not identical before coding.[4] If this happens events belonging to one family may be attributed to another, especially if the marriage concerned took place at the same time. If this occurred in two families both belonging to type MI or MII, fertility rates derived from them would not be affected;[5] but this might happen if one family was of type MI or MII while for the other the date of end of observation was unknown. In that case attributing births occurring in the latter family to the former would cause fertility rates to be overestimated and vice-versa. No instance of identity in the coding of pairs of surnames has been observed so far; but this might happen in villages where brothers often married sisters.

I have assumed implicitly that the reconstitution details of families of type MI and MII obtained by computer would be the same as those produced manually. This is not necessarily so, since a variation in the surnames of a spouse on a burial record might prevent the linking of the burial and marriage records. If this happened, however, it should not introduce bias into the study of fertility (unless name variations were more frequent among migrants and their fertility differed).

[4] This might happen in the following case, for example: BORGNE–TRIBOULET coded as BRN–TRB and BRUNET–TURBOT also coded as BRN–TRB.
[5] But the rates for either type separately might be affected.

E. A. Wrigley and R. S. Schofield

4 Nominal record linkage by computer and the logic of family reconstitution

THE GENERAL PROBLEM

The technique of family reconstitution rests upon a prior logic of nominal record linkage. It is one of several such techniques which have been used increasingly by historians in recent years,[1] and was the first to be defined in a rigorous and systematic way.[2] Since the data sets involved are large and complex and the operations intricate, family reconstitution provides an opportunity to examine many of the logical and technical difficulties which occur in nominal record linkage generally. It can either be carried out by hand or by computer. In what follows we shall suggest solutions to some of the problems encountered in writing algorithms to computerize family reconstitution and shall refer chiefly to English parish registers, though the solutions appear applicable to most vital registration systems.

If everyone were assigned at birth a name which identified him uniquely and was never changed, there could be no ambiguities in reconstructing his life history from a set of records in which each item of information was linked to a name, unless the records had been inaccurately kept.[3] Thus, having found an entry referring to a baptism,

[1] Nominal record linkage between successive censuses, or between census lists and directories, has proved useful in studies of migration and social mobility in the nineteenth century, for example. It has also been used to draw together information from wills, Poor Law Books, tax lists, parish registers, etc. for a variety of historical purposes, or to merge census and vital registration records.

[2] By M. Fleury, and L. Henry, *Des registres paroissiaux à l'histoire de la population. Manuel de dépouillement et d'exploitation de l'état civil ancien* (Paris, 1956).

[3] Inaccuracy might either take the form of failing to use the appropriate character string for the man in question, or recording wrong information linked to the name. For example, a man might be recorded as dying in 1670 aged 83, but the same name might appear in the baptism register in 1632. The two records are incompatible (though

it would only be necessary to search in the marriage and burial registers for records with the same unique character string to discover whether the child whose baptism had been recorded later married or was buried in the area covered by the vital registration system. In these circumstances it would be a relatively simple matter to abstract from the data files all that was known about each individual. The problems would be those associated with establishing the best search procedures to speed the formation of links between items of information referring to the same person.

The name given to a baby at baptism, however, was often not sufficient to identify him uniquely. Indeed the baby was often deliberately given the same name as a parent, grandparent, or other relative sharing the same surname. It is therefore always prudent to consider all the information given at each register entry in the hope that this will enable a confident identification to be made even though the name alone is insufficient. As far as names alone are concerned, a particular burial record, for example, may be linkable to several marriages and baptisms, and unless other information drawn from the records is used, there will be no reason to prefer one link to another.[4]

The range of information in addition to the forename and surname available in each parish register record varies greatly. In the better registers of northern France from the late seventeenth century onwards it is so wide and so consistently recorded that there is seldom any difficulty in deciding, say, whether a marriage record and a burial record on which the names are the same refer to the same person or not.[5] In English parish registers the entries are usually less full and additional information is given less consistently. Most registers, indeed, are so poor that reconstitution is not feasible, or is feasible only for a limited period. There are very few parishes like Colyton where registration was continuous from a very early date (in the case of Colyton from 1538) and the quality of the register, though

---

we may guess that the digits of the age given at death had been accidentally transposed when the record was written), even though the names agree. Since both types of error would be likely to occur occasionally even though great care was taken, it is highly improbable that any large set of records could be kept free from all ambiguities and inconsistencies.

[4] It follows from this, of course, that vital registers in which names alone are recorded are useless for family reconstitution. See E. A. Wrigley, 'Some problems of family reconstitution using English parish register material', *Third International Conference on Economic History*, Munich 1965, Section VII, Demography and Economics, 199–221.

[5] Blayo's chapter illustrates this point by showing how valuable additional information about names can be in this regard.

variable, is sufficiently good to allow reconstitution throughout.[6] In general, in addition to recording the forename and surname of the principal of the record, the head of the family is named and his relationship to the principal defined in baptism records and in burial records where this is appropriate. Sometimes the mother as well as the father is named on baptism and burial records. The parents of the bride and groom are seldom named in marriage records. Occupation and residence are usually recorded only spasmodically, though there are a few registers where one or both were set down quite consistently. Age is rarely recorded, either at marriage or burial until *pro forma* registration became normal (in 1754 for marriages; in 1813 for baptisms and burials[7]).

It will be obvious that if each entry contained information about relationship, age, occupation and residence, given with moderate consistency, it would be exceedingly rare to be in doubt about the identity of any individual named in a register. For example, let us assume that occupation and age are invariably recorded at both marriage and death in a particular register, and that the following records exist (minimum relevant information only included):

1   James Greensmith, butcher, was buried 28 September 1721, aged 58
2   James Greensmith, butcher, aged 27, married Mary Williams, 7 May 1691
3   James Greensmith, husbandman, aged 24, married Jane Horlock, 12 July 1702

There can be no doubt that a link between records 1 and 2 is to be preferred to a link between records 1 and 3. There is only a very small discrepancy in age/date information and agreement in occupation in the first case, whereas in the second the age/date information in the two records does not agree and the occupations differ, though not in a way which would prohibit a link for that reason alone. But suppose that the records lose all age data. The link between records 1 and 2 may still be preferred but the decision must be much less clearcut since it is entirely possible that in the course of a twenty year period

---

[6] The variable quality of the register did, however, pose problems in tabulating and interpreting the results of reconstitution in Colyton. See E. A. Wrigley, 'Family limitation in pre-industrial England', *Economic History Review*, 2nd ser., XIX, no. 1 (1966), 82–109; and 'Mortality in pre-industrial England. The example of Colyton, Devon', Glass and Revelle (eds.), *Population and Social Change* (London, 1972), 244–74.

[7] The changes occurred following Hardwicke's Marriage Act of 1753 and Rose's Act of 1812.

a man might become a butcher rather than a husbandman, or indeed that he had always been both but had been set down differently on the two occasions. If neither age nor occupation is mentioned, there is no immediate reason for preferring one possible link to the other. This does not necessarily mean, however, that the two links are equally likely when the record set as a whole is taken into consideration. For example, there may be a fourth record which resolves the problem:

4   Jane, wife of James Greensmith was buried 10 January 1733

If this record 4 is linkable only to record 3 then it is evident that James Greensmith was still living in 1733 and so could not have died in 1721.

Each incumbent or parish clerk in making entries in the register was guided by his own judgement and by local tradition in deciding how much information to set down beyond the bare minimum of date and name. There are wide variations in usage between different parishes and over time in the same parish.[8] Ages may be given in both marriage and burial records in one period but in neither at another. It is therefore very common in evaluating a possible link between two records to find that the same information field is empty in one record, though filled in another.

When little information is given at each register entry, it will be evident that the number of possible links between records will tend to be large.[9] For example, if the name of the bride and her marital

[8] In some of the big London parishes there was an early tendency towards uniformity of method in entering events in the register, and the entries were not only consistent in form but also frequently quite full, perhaps because the sheer volume of entries induced a bureaucratic turn of mind.

[9] It is interesting that in specifying the rules for manual reconstitution using French registers Fleury and Henry were able largely to ignore the problem of choosing between several possible links. North French registers after 1667 were normally well kept and gave sufficient information at each entry to leave few ambiguities of identification. The difficulty of using poorer French registers is not directly discussed in the Manuel. In essence the logic of the Manuel is that only links about which there is no doubt are to be made, though no explicit definition of conventional certainty is offered (i.e. something which would make it clear what to do when a register lapses briefly from its normal high standard and fails to provide fields of information which are usually recorded). Indeed their text occasionally encourages some latitude in interpreting the rules of reconstitution and scope for personal judgement, which might prove dangerous in unwary hands. They write of the rules for reconstitution, 'Mais leur stricte application ne conduit pas, loin de là, à un travail purement mécanique. L'expérience acquise au cours du dépouillement des registres intervient constamment dans la reconstitution des familles—'. Fleury and Henry, Nouveau manuel de dépouillement et d'exploitation de l'état civil ancien (Paris, 1965), 117. It is true that they make it clear in the same passage that they have chiefly in mind variations in spelling and related

status are all that is stated on a marriage record, it may prove to be linkable to several preceding baptisms, whereas if the names of both her parents are given it is unlikely that there will be more than one baptism to which the marriage can be linked in the baptism file. Since registration practices were so variable even in well-kept English registers, overall record linkage strategy must not be dependent upon full and consistent registration. It must meet three requirements:

1 that every possible link should be considered
2 that it should specify a decision procedure when more than one link can be made from a given record to records of another type (for example, from a burial to several marriages) [10]
3 that the decision procedure should make the best use not simply of the records immediately involved but of all the information in the file as whole which is relevant to the decision.

INTER-RECORD LINKAGE

In family reconstitution five types of inter-record links must be made. They are:

1 BAP–MAR (baptism to marriage)
2 MAR–MAR (marriage to marriage)
3 MAR–BUR (marriage to burial)
4 BAP–BUR (baptism to burial)
5 BAP–MAR [parents] (baptism of child to marriage of parents).

The first four of these five types of linkage are alike and represent sections in the life history of individuals. All four may be made in

---

matters, yet nothing demonstrates more forcibly the excellence of the better French registers than the fact that questions like multiple possible linkage and minimal criteria for linkage obtrude so little into the *Manuel*.

The chapter 'Family reconstitution' in E. A. Wrigley (ed.) *An Introduction to English historical demography* (London, 1966), contains rules for manual reconstitution of English parish registers. In it there is some discussion of the problem of multiple possible linkage. The rules given there prohibit linkage unless a conventional standard of certainty is met (see pp. 132–7). We now think these rules too restrictive, especially when drawing up computer algorithms. For manual operations they may still represent the most prudent course because they are simple to follow. Some of the rules described in this chapter would be virtually impossible to carry out manually.

[10] Links between records of the same type are permissible in only one class of records— marriages. Here there is no restriction upon the number of links which may be formed and later retained, since a man or woman may re-marry several times over.

piecing together the life history of a single man if the records of his baptism, marriage, re-marriage and burial are all to be found in one register. The last is different in nature from the other four since it refers to the allocation of a child to his family of orientation. It differs also in that every baptism which is not illegitimate *must* be linked to a marriage. If an appropriate marriage record does not exist one is created for this purpose (the reasons for this will appear more fully below). All the other types of link are made only when the empirical content of the paired records appears to justify making the link. BAP–MAR [parents] links are similar to other types, on the other hand, inasmuch as any one baptism may be linkable to more than one marriage. There are periods in most baptism registers, for instance, when only the father of the child is named in the baptism entry, so that if there are two or more families present in the parish headed by men bearing the same name, a decision must be made between the possible links.

Given the three prime requirements for record linkage decisions already listed, it might seem that the strategy which should be employed is quite straightforward—first make all the possible links within the five categories of inter-linkage; then, whenever a set of linked records fails a test designed to establish whether or not it refers to one life history only (or in the case of BAP–MAR [parents] links, to one marriage only), frame a suitable algorithm to delete successive links in some ordered way until the record set will past the test. Unhappily, the strategy, though admirable in principle, cannot be adopted in its simple form, though it underlies the more tortuous sequence of operations, made necessary by the characteristics of the parochial registration system and by certain more general constraints.

The sequence of operations entailed in family reconstitution by computer is most conveniently broken down into ten stages:

1   BAP–MAR [parents] linkage
2   MAR–BUR linkage (where the burial record contains reference to a surviving spouse)
3   BAP–MAR [parents] revision (this consists of tests of the inter-genesic intervals in each marriage which ensure that the sequence of birth events is acceptable: it also leaves all baptisms assigned to no more than one marriage)
4   BAP–MAR linkage (the operation which links marriage partners to their baptism records)
5   BAP/MAR–BUR linkage (this deals with all BAP–BUR links and all MAR–BUR links not dealt with in 2)

6   BAP/MAR–BUR revision (a limited set of tests, some of which
     are described below, which set the stage for the last four stages)
7   MAR–MAR linkage (male)
8   RECORD LINKAGE revision (male)
9   MAR–MAR linkage (female)
10   RECORD LINKAGE revision (female)

There are four main considerations which make for some departure
from a system of few and simple stages and result in the ten stages
just listed.

a   Men and women must be treated differently in the final stages
of the program which deals with the revision of record linkages. This
necessity springs from the fact that when an English woman marries
her surname changes. With married women, therefore, unlike
married men, it is never possible to make a link directly from a baptism
to a burial record. This means that some tests which are feasible
within a male record set would be inappropriate in a female record
set. To take a simple example, if a male baptism record is linked to a
marriage which in turn is linked to a burial, but the baptism record
is not linked to the burial, it is immediately certain that one of the
two links must go, since all possible BAP–BUR male links will have
been made in an earlier stage of record linkage. The same would not
be true of a comparable set of female records because no BAP–BUR
links of this type could have been made in a female record set. A
different series of tests is therefore required to determine whether or
not a BAP–BUR link should be created, and so confirm the set of
three records as referring to a single life.

In most of the earlier stages of the program the sex of the individual is noted in deciding whether a link should be made, and in
some the linkage algorithms differ for men and women.

b   In order to ensure that the maximum number of inter-record
links is made, it is obviously necessary to ensure in turn that the
maximum number of records is available when each pair of record
types is treated. If each parish were a closed population and each
event were conscientiously recorded this would not pose any problem. The records which had been input when the register was first
punched would represent the whole relevant record universe. But
since these conditions are never met, in any parish there are always
'ghost' records not to be found in the register but implied by entries
which do exist. For example, if a man and his wife move into a parish,
settle there, raise a family, and ultimately die in it, their burials will
be recorded in the register, though their marriage was not. It is con-

venient in such a case to create a dummy marriage and to place it as a separate record in the marriage file. If this were not done the burial entry which records the death of, say, the husband might be linked unsuitably to a record of another man who was born or married in the parish and who shared the same name but who was not otherwise a likely link. In practice the baptism of children is often the first evidence of the entry of a married couple into a parish and one reason for treating BAP–MAR [parents] links first is the wish to fill up the proper complement of the dummy marriages as early as possible (dummy marriages must be created at the first sign of their existence during the BAP–MAR [parents] linkage phase itself, of course, since failure to do so would restrict the population of marriages to which subsequent baptisms might be linked).

Stage 2 in the sequence of operations, MAR–BUR linkage where the burial record contains reference to a surviving spouse, is placed early for the same reason. It sometimes happens that when a man's wife dies, he remarries quickly[11] taking his new wife from another parish and marrying her there before bring her back to live in his own parish. If baptism entries take the simple form, 'William, son of Henry Johnson, was baptised (date)', the flow of baptisms recorded in the register will provide no clue to what has occurred because the mother's forename is not entered when the baptism of her child is set down. Making use of the first wife's burial record prevents all the baptisms being linked to one marriage record. A dummy marriage is created to take Henry Johnson's later children and to enable the burial entry of his second wife to be allocated appropriately. To provide wherever possible a firm date for the end of each marriage, therefore, all burial entries which take the form 'x., wife of $y.z.$' (or the parallel form '$y.z.$, husband of x.', should it occur) are dealt with early. Burial entries in this form imply relatively strong links because links will be made only when there is a double forename match of both husband and wife. If there is any ambiguity about a MAR–BUR link in stage 2 because a burial is linkable to more than one marriage, or a marriage linkable to more than one such burial, the ambiguity is resolved in this stage by match-scoring rather than being left to the final stages of record linkage revision.[12] Because links of this type are relatively strong it is unlikely that any incompatible link of greater

---

[11] Men tended to remarry more quickly than women, though the mean interval between death of spouse and remarriage lengthened considerably for both sexes between the sixteenth and eighteenth centuries. In the sixteenth many men had remarried within three months of their previous wife's death and marriages within less than a month were not unknown.

[12] The method of matchscoring used is described in a later section of this article.

strength will come to light at a later stage in record linkage.[13]

There are circumstances also in which dummy baptisms must be created, notably when a child is buried soon after birth without having been baptized (the burial of a stillborn child is a special variant of this case: in some parishes the burials of stillborn children appear to have been regularly entered in the registers over long periods.)

c   Decisions may have to be made about one type of link before another can be formed. For example, one of the conventional requirements to be met before a spouse can remarry is that there should be evidence that his or her partner had died before the date of the new marriage.[14] The date of death of the spouse marks the re-entry of the survivor into the marriage market. Until this is known MAR–MAR linkage cannot take place since no bound can be put to the time span within which links can properly be sought. In English parish registers when a woman died while her husband was still living, it was common practice to record both her name and her husband's in the burial register. But when a husband died in similar circumstances his name alone was normally set down and not his wife's. The first type of entry gives rise to stronger links than the second, other things being equal, since the former involves a double name match, while the latter involves only a single name match. In resolving complex and conflicting sets of links, therefore, the burial records of wives provide more 'leverage' than those of husbands. This is the main reason why it is more convenient to take MAR–MAR linkage for men first and then to revise male record linkage generally before carrying out the parallel operations for women.

d   The sense in which BAP–MAR [parents] linkage differs from the other four types of record linkage has already been discussed. BAP–MAR [parents] linkage decisions do not affect linkage decisions in the sets of links built up by the other four linkage processes in any direct way but there are problems of consistency within the universe of BAP–MAR [parents] links and there are more subtle ways in which the implications of BAP–MAR [parents] decisions must be taken into account (one has already been described in connection with the creation of dummy marriages).

Stage 3 consists of a set of tests to ascertain whether any baptisms have been linked to parents' marriages at dates which would imply a clash with other BAP–MAR [parents] links in the same marriage

[13] It is possible that an existing BAP–MAR [parents] link in which both parents are named will prove equally strong or stronger. The algorithm used includes a test for the existence of BAP–MAR [parents] links which conflict with the wife's burial record. The MAR–BUR link and the conflicting BAP–MAR [parents] link(s) are then matchscored.

[14] Divorce is ignored in this program. It was extremely rare in the parish register period.

because the intergenesic intervals involved are too short to be credible. At the same time the multiple allocation of the same baptism to more than one marriage is resolved by a matchscoring procedure.

Further down the sequence of operations in stage 6 the consistency of BAP–MAR [parents] linkages is tested again in view of the BUR–BAP links made for children in the previous stage. When a child was buried, the name of his father or of both his parents was recorded. So children's burial records as well as their baptism entries contain evidence of the continued survival of the parents or of their demise. This evidence must be consistent. It is unacceptable, for example, to have one child buried in, say 1630, as '*r.* son of *x.z.*, widow' while another child in the same family is buried in 1633 as '*p.* daughter of *y.z.* and his wife *x.*'. Stage 6 contains algorithms to deal with any inconsistencies of this type which may be detected. At the same time it is possible to reduce some of the complexity of links of other types. This is particularly true of links relating to the burial of husbands. These are usually particularly weak links since it was quite common when a husband died to enter only his name and date of his burial in the register. The much stronger links made at the burial of his children where there are often three accordant names in the linked records (child, father and mother) may establish clearly that the father was still living up to a certain date, and so enable MAR–BUR links which would imply that he had died before that date to be deleted.[15] This too is done at stage 6.

DEMOGRAPHIC CONSTRAINTS UPON RECORD LINKAGE

It is the general purpose of the early stages of family reconstitution program to allow links to be formed as freely as possible so that in the final revision stages decisions can be taken with the maximum amount of information available for review. Certain restrictions upon this overall strategy have just been described. In addition to these restrictions, which spring from the nature of the English parochial registration system, there are other constraints of a more general nature. They are mainly demographic, and while some details of the rules listed may be disputed, they would have to be paralleled in any

---

[15] This is a simplified account of the tests involved, meant only to suggest the logic of the process. The full algorithm is rather complex and takes account of other types of record link which taken altogether improve the accuracy of the final decision.

record linkage program which used a vital registration series in which there were problems of identification because many records had only a few information fields. The rules serve to prevent the formation of spurious links or to identify false links during revision. Together they form a set of conventional rules whose provisions are intended to allow the overwhelming bulk of true links to be formed while at the same time preventing the formation of a mass of links whose presence would be a handicap in the later stages of the program when choices must be made between competing links.[16] For example, a few women will bear children above the age of 50 but to relax the second rule listed by substituting 55 for 50 as the upper age limit might produce an unacceptable number of wrong linkages of births to women at an advanced age.[17]

1   Age at death is never greater than 100 years, unless age information in the burial record overrides this rule.

2   At the birth of a child the mother is never less than 15 or more than 50 years old, nor the father less than 15 or more than 75.

3   No two successive birth events to the same mother occur in less than 10 months and no three successive birth events in less than 22 months.[18]

4   The interval between the end of a marriage and the remarriage of the surviving spouse must be less than 20 years.

5   First marriages (for both sexes) occur only when the bride or groom is above 15 years of age and less than 50, unless age information in the marriage record overrides the rule.

6   All brides and grooms are less than 75 years of age at marriage unless age information in the marriage record overrides the rule.

---

[16] There are a few further constraints of minor importance which relate to the oddities of English parochial registration. They do not warrant examination here.

[17] It is, of course, a simple matter to relax all of the assumptions to do with maximum or minimum ages at death, marriage birth of child, etc., and then to run the program on a body of data which has already been subjected to the program in its more restrictive form. If it should then appear that the fear of a substantial number of wrong linkages is unfounded, the conventional limits can be modified.

[18] Since in many cases a date of baptism only is known and the interval between birth and baptism may vary from a few hours to a matter of months, this convention is less easy to apply than might initially appear, especially as the date of baptism or birth, if given, may not be known exactly. On input a system of weighting is used to indicate the degree of imprecision with which an event is dated (where weight 0 implies no imprecision and the higher the number, the greater the uncertainty). The algorithm which covers the third rule includes a subroutine which takes account both of any imprecision of dating and of the problem of the interval between birth and baptism and sets two dates for each baptism between which the true date is regarded as lying. The date is then allowed to 'float' between these limits during testing if necessary.

7   Whenever an age is given in either one or both of the records involved in a possible link the difference between the dates of the two records must be compatible with the age information given.
8   Where occupations are stated in both records involved in a possible link and they mismatch in a manner which is thought to be incompatible even with the most extreme assumptions about lifetime occupational mobility, no link is made (for example, labourer/vicar).
9   In addition to the requirement that the names of the principal on two records should agree before a link is made, there must also be no disagreement in the names of any relatives named in both records (for example, if the names of both parents are recorded at the baptism of a child, and again when he is buried, they must not disagree if a BAP–BUR link is to be made).

In this connection it should be emphasized that the question of whether or not a pair of names agree is of fundamental importance since the decisions taken on this issue divide up the universe of records into comparison sets within which all later operations take place. This question is discussed at greater length in the appendix to this article.

CLUSTERS AND CHAINS

The record links which build up during stages 1–7 and 9 take the form of the exchange of addresses between all pairs of records which satisfy the minimum set of conditions and constraints just described. In many surname/forename sets of records, and especially where the sets are small or most records contain abundant information, there will be little to do in stages 8 and 10 when record linkages are reviewed and revised. In such surname/forename sets the vast majority of individual life histories contain few or no ambiguities to be resolved. But the program must also cater for situations in which many links have been made which are not compatible with each other, and some must be deleted if the mass of links is to be resolved into a series of life histories.

The difficulties which require resolution fall into two main classes, those of incompatibility and those of multiplicity. Incompatibility occurs when record A is linked to record B, and record B is linked to record C, but there is no link between A and C, in spite of the fact that they are of different types and may properly be linked if certain minimum conditions are met. A simple illustration of this situation is shown in Figure 1. In this illustration it is immediately obvious why

Figure 1

the burial and baptism are not linked since they are separated by more than 100 years and are therefore outside the conventional time limits for a link of this type. Incompatibility, however, may take many forms. For example, there may be a BAP–BUR link and a MAR–BUR link, but no BAP–MAR link (perhaps because the parents of the bride and groom are named in the marriage record and do not agree with the parents named in the baptism record). This is the situation represented schematically in Figure 2.

Figure 2

Any set of linked records which purports to relate to a single life must at some stage in the program pass a crucial test, *that each record in the set is linked to every other and that no record in the set is linked to any record outside the set.* Until this condition is satisfied the set of records must be modified by a selective deletion of links which will eventually enable the test to be passed. Any set of linked records which contains an incompatibility will fail this test until the incompatibility is removed. In the case shown in figure 1, for example, whichever is the weaker of the BAP–MAR and MAR–BUR links will be deleted. When this has been done the incompatibility disappears.

The multiplicity problem will also invariably be detected by the test just described. It is illustrated by Figure 3. No single life history

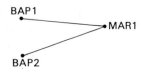

Figure 3

can contain more than one baptism or burial record, though it may contain two or more marriages. Therefore, until one of the two BAP–MAR links in the Figure 3 has been deleted the test will continue to be failed.

The decision process in sets of linked records which contain incompatibilities or multiplicities may be made more complex by the existence of backtracks within the record set. This expression is meant to cover the type of situation shown in Figure 4. In a record

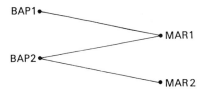

Figure 4

set without backtracks what has usually to be resolved is essentially the life history of one man or woman. The uncertainty may take many forms (which of several possibilities is the right burial record to link to a particular baptism; which of several baptisms ought to be linked to a given marriage; etc.) but in most cases it centres round a single life. When the uncertainty has been resolved there will usually remain a scatter of individual records left unlinked as well as a linked set which represent an individual life history (there are some exceptions to this generalization). If there is a backtrack in the configuration, however, more individuals will commonly be involved and substantial parts of the life histories of two or more people may remain after linkage revision. In the example shown in Figure 4, for instance, the deletion of the BAP2–MAR1 link leaves sections of the life histories of two people and no further incompatibilities or multiplicities to be resolved. The deletion of either of the other two links, however, would leave a multiplicity unresolved and mean an eventual solution in which a section of only one life history remains plus two unlinked records.

There is no limit in principle to the extent of the backtracks within any single surname set of linked records so that the algorithms which revise record links in the late stages of the program must be capable of dealing with all possible combinations of incompatibilities, multiplicities and backtracks in any given set of linked records.

Before any complex set of linkages can be resolved in stages 8 and 10 of the sequence of operations, the extent of each set of linked records must first be determined. Once this has been done, individual life histories within each set are traced out. It is convenient to refer to the set of linked records as a cluster and to the life histories into which it is decomposed as chains. The links within a chain are, of course, links between pairs of records, such as BAP–MAR or a MAR–BUR link, which together represent what is known of the vital events in the life of a single individual. Once the chains have been formed it is a comparatively simple matter to rearrange the information present in the chains into the form made familiar by family reconstitution carried out by hand, since any offspring of a marriage are already uniquely linked to it by stages 1 and 3 of the program and the marriage record will also contain links to all the records which comprise the chains of the husband and wife. The chains of any category of kin can be reached by appropriate search algorithms.

The record links within a chain may have arisen or been confirmed for any one of three reasons. First, a link may be present because it is regarded as certain in terms of the linkage conventions used. This means that no multiplicities or incompatibilities ever affected the pair of records involved in the link. Their relationship was always one-to-one; there was never any reason in the light of the evidence available to doubt the validity of the link.[19] Second, a link may occur in a chain because it was a winner in a matchscoring competition which was necessary in order to resolve the cluster into a chain or chains. One or both records in the link had at some stage been linked to records not present in the chain as it was ultimately constituted.[20] Third, a link may have been retained in a chain following a process of random allocation between two or more conflicting links of equal strength. Each link within a chain is flagged to indicate the type of decision which caused it to be accepted (certain, matchscore winner, random allocation). This makes it possible later when tabulating the data to include or exclude information according to the type of decision which brought about the link. For example, the tabulation of age of marriage, which is based upon BAP–MAR links, can be made to include links of all three types, or each type can be tabulated separately, or indeed any combination of types may be used, depending on the purpose of the tabulation.

---

[19] This does not necessarily mean, of course, that the link is intrinsically a very strong one with agreement over a wide range of information fields in the two records. In a limiting case the agreement may have been no more than a simple nominal match. It does mean, however, that there was not at any stage a conflicting link which was later deleted.

[20] A link of this type may nevertheless be intrinsically very strong if the agreement between the two records covers several information fields while the conflicting links were all weak.

RECORD LINKAGE REVISION

In order to follow the successive steps of record linkage revision it is convenient to begin by describing the process of cluster formation. Clusters are formed by reading in successively all the records which comprise a surname/forename set. If a record contains no addresses of other records in its address register it cannot form part of a cluster and calls for no action.[21] It represents an isolated event, say the burial of a recent migrant into the parish, of whom nothing else is known. If, on the other hand, the current record is linked to other records a search is made to discover whether the current record or any record to which it is linked is to be found among the records already listed in an existing cluster. If so the current record is added to the cluster. If the records in the register of the current record are to be found in two or more clusters then all the clusters in question are consolidated into a single cluster and the current record is added to it. It may be, of course, that there is no record common to the address registers of the current record and of any existing cluster. In this case the current record becomes the first record in a new cluster which is then placed in a file of clusters.

Each cluster, when complete, forms a self-contained record universe which must comprise all the information which is relevant to the breaking down of the cluster into a number of chains.[22] Record linkage revision, therefore, will use the set of completed clusters as the units within which to operate. The definition of clusters is an essential preliminary to the formation or confirmation of chains.

The basic test which defines the existence of a chain has already been given—that each record is linked to every other in the chain and that no record in the chain is linked to any record not in the chain. Accordingly, the first test to be made upon a cluster is whether it already satisfies this condition, whether, that is to say, all the linked records assembled in the cluster refer to one man. In many cases, where a cluster contains only a small number of records (usually, two, three or four), the condition is met immediately. But where the surname set contains many records, or a high proportion of the records

[21] For completeness' sake it should be noted that BAP–MAR [parents] links are ignored here. They link an individual to his or her family of orientation but they do not form part of any chain and are not 'read' during cluster formation.

[22] There is a minor gloss to this statement which is perhaps worth noting. The chains formed in stage 8—the life histories of men in a parish—may have repercussions outside the cluster in which they were formed, because the linking of male burials to marriages, in cases where the husband dies before the wife, frees her to remarry, and account will be taken of this in stages 9 and 10. In this case therefore, a decision taken in a particular cluster may have an effect outside it.

contain only a few fields of information, or both, the earlier stages of the program will tend to produce a large number of links, and in-compatibilities, multiplicities and backtracks may abound. Many links may have to be deleted before the criterion for the existence of an acceptable chain is met.

A description of the decomposition of a cluster into its component chains will serve to clarify the logic and the operational sequences involved in the course of record linkage revision. In Figure 5 the

	BAP1	BAP2	BAP3	MAR1	MAR2	MAR3	MAR4	BUR1	BUR2	BUR3	BUR4
BAP1	0	0	0	1	1	1	0	1	1	1	0
BAP2	0	0	0	1	1	1	1	1	1	0	1
BAP3	0	0	0	0	0	1	0	1	1	0	0
MAR1	0	0	0	0	1	1	0	1	1	1	0
MAR2	0	0	0	0	0	0	0	0	1	0	0
MAR3	0	0	0	0	0	0	0	0	0	0	1
MAR4	0	0	0	0	0	0	0	0	0	0	1
BUR1	0	0	0	0	0	0	0	0	0	0	0
BUR2	0	0	0	0	0	0	0	0	0	0	0
BUR3	0	0	0	0	0	0	0	0	0	0	0
BUR4	0	0	0	0	0	0	0	0	0	0	0

$A =$ (label to the left of the matrix)

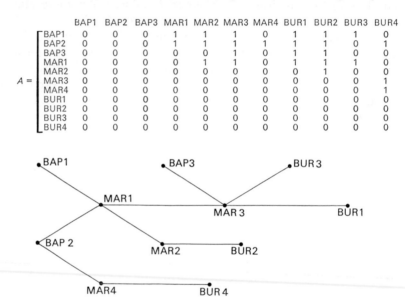

Figure 5

cluster is shown as an adjacency matrix. In it the presence of a 1 in any cell represents the existence of a link between the two records of the row and column concerned, (for example, BAP1–MAR1) while a 0 indicates the absence of a link. Since all records are dated, any pair of records can be ordered in time. The presence of a 1 in a cell therefore also shows the direction of the link (earlier to later). The diagram below the adjacency matrix provides a visual sketch of the structure of the cluster, but only a fraction of the links are shown since to include them all would result in a pattern of lines too numer-ous to be easy to grasp. Even the diagram shows, however, that there are several multiplicities in the cluster and an obvious back-track involving BAP1, BAP2, MAR1 and MAR4. But the information con-tained in the matrix also reveals other problems within the cluster which cannot be inferred directly from the diagram. For example, the absence of a link BAP2–BUR3 would mean that if BAP2–MAR1 –MAR3 proved to be a preferred part chain, the final link would have to include BUR1 rather than BUR3 since BUR3 and BAP2 are incompatible.

In every cluster there must be one or more chains waiting to be defined. In order to follow the successive operations involved it is convenient to convert the adjacency matrix (A) shown in Figure 5 into a reachability matrix (R). This conversion is of great importance because of the character of female record clusters. For example, it may happen in the course of building up inter-record links that a female BAP–MAR link is formed, and also a MAR–BUR link concerning the same marriage (both are 'adjacent' links), but there can be no BAP–BUR link because of the change of name at marriage. It is essential to discover whether the burial is 'reachable' from the baptism, and if so to form the BAP–BUR link. This is already known in the case of a male cluster since all possible links will already have been formed. For this reason, with a male record cluster matrix (R) is the same as matrix (A) except that each cell on the main diagonal is set to 1 (each record being reachable from itself). The matrix (A) shown in Figure 5, is of course, a male cluster. In order to make the subsequent tests and operations easier to follow, it is convenient, but neither logically nor operationally necessary, to add to the reachability matrix its transpose (R') to form the matrix $(R + R')$. The transpose of a matrix is formed by reversing the direction of every line represented in it (i.e. if in matrix $(R)r_{ij} = 1$, in its transpose $(R')r_{ji} = 1$). Figure 6 shows the same cluster as Figure 5 but in the

	BAP1	BAP2	BAP3	MAR1	MAR2	MAR3	MAR4	BUR1	BUR2	BUR3	BUR4
BAP1	1	0	0	1	1	1	0	1	1	1	0
BAP2	0	1	0	1	1	1	1	1	1	0	1
BAP3	0	0	1	0	0	1	0	1	1	0	0
MAR1	1	1	0	1	1	1	0	1	1	1	0
MAR2	1	1	0	1	1	0	0	0	1	0	0
MAR3	1	1	1	1	0	1	0	1	0	1	0
MAR4	0	1	0	0	0	0	1	0	0	0	1
BUR1	1	1	1	1	1	0	1	0	1	0	0
BUR2	1	1	1	1	1	0	0	0	1	0	0
BUR3	1	0	0	1	0	1	0	0	0	1	0
BUR4	0	1	0	0	0	0	1	0	0	0	1

$(R+R')=$

Figure 6

form of a matrix $(R + R')$. It will serve to show how chains are teased out of clusters. The additional operations necessary with a female cluster are described later.

The first step to be taken is to test whether the group of records in the cluster already constitutes a chain. If the cluster is itself a chain, there will be a 1 in every cell. This is the matrix representation of the rule that every record is linked to every other in a chain (there can be no link to a record outside the cluster since by definition it has no external links).

The cluster shown in matrix form in Figure 6 is clearly not a chain. The scattering of 0's reflects the many multiplicities, incompatibilities, and backtracks in the cluster. Only when the pattern of 0's and 1's in the rows of two or more linked records is identical can a chain begin to be proved. Lack of identity in the rows of any linked pair of records means either that record A is linked to a record to which record B is not linked (if there is a 1 in row A in a column in which there is a 0 in row B), or that record A is not linked to a record to which record B is linked, in the reverse case. Only the deletion of some existing links, and the accompanying disappearance of multiplicities, incompatibilities and backtracks, can produce one or more chains from the cluster.[23]

The problem therefore becomes that of choosing the links to be deleted. In a state of uncertainty it is reasonable to work outwards from the most certain available evidence and begin with the individual link in which the greatest confidence can be placed. The next step, therefore, is to determine the strongest link. The link need not be between 'adjacent' records; for example, it may be a BAP–BUR link, where each record is also linked to an intervening marriage record. In the present example, let us assume that the MAR1–MAR3 link is the strongest. It now becomes the basis for the formulation and testing of a chain, using the 'leverage' which the identification of the strongest link affords.

After finding the strongest link, any links which conflict with it are deleted. If record A and record B possess the strongest link then any

[23] It will be obvious that the foregoing can be readily restated in the terminology of digraph theory, which offers a number of concepts valuable for the clarification of the operations involved in reducing clusters to chains. Reachability is one such concept.
   The following points are worth noting:
1   All reconstitution digraphs are asymmetric.
2   A chain is a complete, asymmetric and transitive digraph, whereas a cluster, though asymmetric, lacks either completeness or transitivity or both.
3   A chain has exactly one transmitter which is a unique source, and exactly one receiver which is a unique sink. Clusters may have several transmitters and receivers.
4   In a chain all records are 2-connected. In a cluster any backtrack or multiplicity will mean that some records are 1-connected. Incompatible records are sometimes 1-connected; where this is not so there will be an absence of transitivity.
5   A chain is a unilateral subgraph of a cluster digraph; or, in matrix terminology, a unilateral submatrix of a cluster matrix.
See F. Harary, R. Z. Norman, D. Cartwright, *Structural models* (New York, London, Sydney, 1965).

link from record A to a record which is not linked to record B must be deleted, and similarly if record B is linked to any records not linked to record A, then these links too must go. In the present instance, the links MAR1–MAR2 and MAR1–BUR2 are deleted since MAR3 is not linked either to MAR2 or BUR2 and a similar operation on MAR3 results in deletion of the MAR3–BAP3 link. This is equivalent to deleting any multiplicity or incompatibility as far as these two records are concerned and also isolates them from any backtracks. Represented in a matrix $(R + R')$ this reduces to a very simple operation. The MAR1 and MAR3 rows must be made to read identically. Wherever they do not, the discrepant 1 is replaced by an 0. Thus the MAR2 and BUR2 cells on the MAR1 row becomes 0's, as does also the BAP3 cell on the MAR3 line (for each r_{ij} deletion there is also a r_{ji} deletion). This first round of deletions is shown by underlining the deleted 1's in Figure 6.

The records which prove to be common to the address registers of the pair of records connected by the strongest link are then set in a common register. They can be read off from the 1's on either the MAR1 or MAR3 rows.

Common register (1) BAP1 BAP2 MAR1 MAR3 BUR1 BUR3

Finding the strongest link has identified one link in the chain. The common register lists the other records linked to the two records of the strongest link, and therefore contains the set of records from amongst which the chain will eventually be defined. It is possible that the deletions already made will have produced a chain. Therefore the prime test is repeated at this stage to ascertain whether each record in the common register contains the address of every other and to make sure that no address not found in the common register is present in any common register record. If the test is passed the pattern of 1's and 0's will be identical on the rows of all the common register records. The rows of the records in the common register may be moved to the top of the matrix as soon as it has been established, so that their dissimilarities, if any, are more easily picked out.

Clearly the test is not yet passed. For example, BAP1 is not linked to BAP2 though both are in the common register, and BAP1 is linked to BUR2 though the latter is not listed in the common register. More deletions must be made to produce a chain.

At this stage, in addition to the common register, it is convenient to create a strongest link register consisting initially in this instance of MAR1–MAR3.

Once the two registers have been established the sequence of operations takes the form of a cycle which ceases when a chain has been established. The sequence is the following:

1   Establish the common register and the strongest link register.
2   Test for the existence of a chain.
3   Test for the existence of a link from any common register record A to a non-common register record which is stronger than any link from record A to a record in the strongest link register. If such a link exists, the links between record A and all the strongest link register records are deleted and record A is removed from the common register. This is done following the principle that a stronger link in competition with a weaker should always have preference, but the fewest possible deletions are made to avoid prejudicing future action. Record A cannot remain in the common register since it has a stronger external link but links are deleted only to records in the strongest link register, which are certain to form part of the chain which is being established. If such a link exists the program returns to stage 2; if it does not it moves to stage 4.
4   The strongest link between any two common register records (other than those already in the strongest link register) is identified, and added to the strongest link register. The rows of all records in this register must be made to read identically, just as in the case of the initial strongest link pair. This may, but need not necessarily, also modify the common register. This stage is concerned both with the external and internal links of the strongest link register. Making the rows identical may mean both deleting links to non-common register records (external) and to common register records (internal), or to either one of the two. The program then returns to stage 2. Sooner or later the test at stage 2 will be passed and a chain established.

In the current example the stage 3 test will show the following external links from common register records.

BAP1–MAR2 and BAP1–BUR2
BAP2–MAR2, BAP2–MAR4, BAP2–BUR2 and BAP2–BUR4
BAP3–BUR1

MAR1 and MAR3 have no such links by definition as a result of the first round of deletions, while BUR3, as it so happens has links exclusively within the common register.

Let us suppose that the links BAP2–MAR4 is stronger than any link between BAP2 and a common register record. This will entail the deletion of the BAP2–MAR1 and BAP2–MAR3 links. The deletions are indicated by the symbol ⌐ in Figure 6 and produce the matrix shown in Figure 7. If this is the only external link which calls

		MAR1	MAR3	BAP1	BUR1	BUR3	BAP2	BAP3	MAR2	MAR4	BUR2	BUR4
	MAR1	1	1	1	1	1	0	0	0	0	0	0
	MAR3	1	1	1	$\bar{1}$	1	0	0	0	0	0	0
	BAP1	1	1	1	$\bar{1}$	1	0	0	1⌐	0	1⌐	0
	BUR1	1	1	1	$\bar{1}$	0	1	1	$\bar{0}$	0	$\bar{0}$	0
$(R+R')=$	BUR3	$\bar{1}$	$\bar{1}$	$\bar{1}$	0	1	0	0	0	0	0	0
	BAP2	0	0	0	1	0	1	0	1	1	1	1
	BAP3	0	0	0	1	0	0	1	0	0	1	0
	MAR2	0	0	1⌐	0	0	1	0	1	0	1	0
	MAR4	0	0	$\bar{0}$	0	0	1	0	0	1	0	1
	BUR2	0	0	1⌐	0	0	1	1	1	0	1	0
	BUR4	0	0	$\bar{0}$	0	0	1	0	0	1	0	1

Figure 7

for action, the common register can be redefined with the deletion of BAP2 (i.e. its disappearance from the MAR1 and MAR3 rows), and the program returns to stage 2.

Common register (2)   BAP1   MAR1   MAR3   BUR1   BUR3

The test for the existence of a chain is again failed. It is clear at a glance that the pattern of 1's and 0's is still not identical on all the rows of common register records. There are still links between common register records and outside records, and not all common register records are mutually addressed (BUR1 and BUR3 cannot both survive in the same chain for this reason).

Assume that the program on this cycle passes through stage 3 without action[24] and that MAR1–BUR3 proves to be the strongest link between common register records found in stage 4. This in effect adds BUR3 to MAR1 and MAR3 as rows within the matrix which must be made identical with each other by replacing discrepant 1's with 0's and produces a new common register. The deletions are shown underlined in Figure 7.

Common register (3)   BAP1   MAR1   MAR3   BUR3

[24] Action will seldom be needed in the second and later cycles but it may occasionally be necessary since the common register is no longer the same as that used during the first cycle and it is possible that an external link which was weaker than a link to a then existing common register record will prove to be stronger than any link to a record still in the common register.

A further recycling is necessary because the stage 2 test shows that the common register records still do not possess identical rows (BAP1 still has external links). If, however, at stage 4 BAP1–MAR1 proves the strongest link between the common register records the situation is finally clarified since the same procedure used before now produces the deletions shown by the symbol ⌋ in Figure 7. Figure 8 shows the final position.

		MAR1	MAR3	BAP1	BUR3	BAP2	BAP3	MAR2	MAR4	BUR1	BUR2	BUR4
	MAR1	1	1	1	1	0	0	0	0	0	0	0
	MAR3	1	1	1	1	0	0	0	0	0	0	0
	BAP1	1	1	1	1	0	0	0	0	0	0	0
	BUR3	1	1	1	1	0	0	0	0	0	0	0
	BAP2	0	0	0	0	1	0	1	1	1	1	1
$(R+R')=$	BAP3	0	0	0	0	0	1	0	0	1	1	0
	MAR2	0	0	0	0	1	0	1	0	0	1	0
	MAR4	0	0	0	0	1	0	0	1	0	0	1
	BUR1	0	0	0	0	1	0	0	1	0	0	0
	BUR2	0	0	0	0	1	1	1	0	0	1	0
	BUR4	0	0	0	0	1	0	0	1	0	0	1

Figure 8

Within the submatrix formed by BAP1, MAR1, MAR3 and BUR3 all the records are linked to each other and none is linked to any outside record. They represent the life history of one man. The pattern of links still remaining among the other records in the original cluster is also easy to pick out, and after the records forming the sub-matrix have been removed from the matrix since they are now confirmed as a chain, the remaining matrix can be processed exactly like the original matrix and so on until all the chains contained in it have been established.

FEMALE RECORD LINKAGE REVISION

We may now turn to consider the additional operations necessary with a female record cluster in which the reachability matrix may be very different from the adjacency matrix because of the change of name at marriage. In the adjacency matrix shown in Figure 9 for example, it is quite possible that BAP1 and BUR1 refer to the same woman.

		BAP1	BAP2	MAR1	MAR2	BUR1	BUR2
	BAP1	0	0	1	0	0	0
	BAP2	0	0	1	0	0	0
$A =$	MAR1	0	0	0	1	0	0
	MAR2	0	0	0	0	1	1
	BUR1	0	0	0	0	0	0
	BUR2	0	0	0	0	0	0

Figure 9

In order to overcome this limitation, imposed by English social convention, boolean arithmetic may be used to discover how many marriages and burials are reachable from each baptism, and so on. R_0 is the matrix of points reachable in o steps from each point (and will therefore consist simply of a series of 1s on the main diagonal). R_1 is the matrix of points reachable in 1 step (formed by adding the adjacency matrix A to R_0); R_2 that reachable in two steps; R_3 in 3 steps; and so on. By iteration the reachability characteristics of any matrix can be established. In a female reconstitution matrix the largest possible number of steps is (1 (baptism) + total number of marriages + 1 (burial)) − 1, and in practice a stable situation is usually reached in fewer steps than this if the matrix is large.

Each of the series of matrices can be generated from the previous one by matrix multiplication of the form $\sum_{k=1}^{n} a_{ik}b_{kj}$. Reachability at each stage is established by successively raising the power of the adjacency matrix: the nth power of the adjacency matrix will show how many records can be reached in n steps or fewer from each record in the matrix. R_2 is shown in figure 10 and R_3 in Figure 11.

$$
R_2 = \begin{array}{c|cccccc}
 & \text{BAP1} & \text{BAP2} & \text{MAR1} & \text{MAR2} & \text{BUR1} & \text{BUR2} \\
\hline
\text{BAP1} & 1 & 0 & 1 & 1 & 0 & 0 \\
\text{BAP2} & 0 & 1 & 1 & 1 & 0 & 0 \\
\text{MAR1} & 0 & 0 & 1 & 1 & 1 & 1 \\
\text{MAR2} & 0 & 0 & 0 & 1 & 1 & 1 \\
\text{BUR1} & 0 & 0 & 0 & 0 & 1 & 0 \\
\text{BUR2} & 0 & 0 & 0 & 0 & 0 & 1 \\
\end{array}
$$

Figure 10

$$
R_3 = \begin{array}{c|cccccc}
 & \text{BAP1} & \text{BAP2} & \text{MAR1} & \text{MAR2} & \text{BUR1} & \text{BUR2} \\
\hline
\text{BAP1} & 1 & 0 & 1 & 1 & 1 & 1 \\
\text{BAP2} & 0 & 1 & 1 & 1 & 1 & 1 \\
\text{MAR1} & 0 & 0 & 1 & 1 & 1 & 1 \\
\text{MAR2} & 0 & 0 & 0 & 1 & 1 & 1 \\
\text{BUR1} & 0 & 0 & 0 & 0 & 1 & 0 \\
\text{BUR2} & 0 & 0 & 0 & 0 & 0 & 1 \\
\end{array}
$$

Figure 11

Figure 11 shows the stable reachability situation (i.e. R_4 would be identical with R_3). This procedure of course, is not applicable in its full simplicity to a female cluster because of a problem which has already been discussed—that there can be no automatic assumption of transitivity in a female cluster. Thus for example, a BAP may be linked to a MAR which is in turn linked to a BUR but yet no link between the BAP and the BUR may be admissible. Therefore at each stage in extending the reachability matrix the mutual consistency of the two records, now about to be declared reachable one from the other, must be checked, using the appropriate tests from the earlier parts of the linkage program. If no link can legitimately be made the matrix entry must $= 0$. The stable situation may therefore contain fewer 1's in the matrix than in a more conventional reachability matrix. Once it has been defined, however, exactly the same algorithm used to create chains for men from the $(R + R')$ matrix can be used for women. Chains for women are therefore established in the same way as for men once the reachability operations have created a comparable matrix situation.

MATCHSCORING

The matrix operations which resolve clusters into chains depend upon discovering the strongest link within a cluster and then using this knowledge as a means of reducing the complexity of the pattern of links. By iteration this will reduce the cluster to a number of chains in the manner just described. Clearly therefore, the method by which the relative strength of the links composing a cluster is assessed determines the final result of the process of record linkage revision.

To establish the relative strengths of the links within a cluster, a system of scoring link strengths must be specified. Several strategies are possible. For example, since each record within a cluster will contain a number of information fields, that link might be held strongest where the information fields of the two records concerned agree in the largest number of cases. In other words, the degree of confidence to be placed in a link is made to depend upon the amount of evidence available that the two records concerned refer to the same person, and agreement or disagreement on each information field is the criterion used.

In a very simple system positive agreement between parallel information fields might score 1, positive disagreement -1, and other possible combinations 0 (for example, where information is missing from either record). Or the scoring system might be made more sensitive by a system of weighting. For instance, a positive agreement in the name of a relative listed in both records might be scored higher than a positive agreement on place of residence. Equally, within the same information field weighting of scores is possible. Bell-founding was a rare occupation. If, therefore, a positive match in the occupation field is found in two records in which the principal is described as a bell-founder, it might be scored more highly than a similar match where the occupation in question was that of labourer, since the latter has a greater chance of arising by coincidence.

Scoring systems in which all fields of information are considered simultaneously, however, often suffer from a major drawback. This is so whenever there is an implicit assumption that agreement between parallel information fields enhances the likelihood of the link, and that disagreement carries the opposite implication. If men always lived in the places in which they were born and never changed their jobs, this would be a reasonable assumption. When this is not the case a system developed round this assumption entails the danger that stay-at-homes who stick to the same job will tend to outscore those who move from place to place or change their occupation. As a result the resolution of clusters may be distorted and, inasmuch as occupational mobility and migration are themselves the objects of study, the information provided by family reconstitution runs the risk of being biased. An alternative strategy to that in which all fields are considered simultaneously, and which might be termed probabilistic in intent, is to examine information fields successively, in a manner which might be called preferential. This is the solution which we have adopted.

Names are less likely to change than any other type of information given in a vital record. That this is so is implicit in the use of surnames to subdivide the whole universe of records into comparison sets. In a preferential system therefore, full use is made of names before having recourse to other types of information. In the initial linking stage of the program a match between the surnames and forenames on any two records is a prerequisite of linkage. At that stage all parallel name fields in the pair of records are examined and a positive mismatch prevents linkage (for example, if the father of the principal on the two records is named in both but in one is John and in the other William, this acts as a bar to linkage). At the stage of matchscoring parallel name fields are again examined and positive matches are scored. If one link within the cluster outscores all the rest, it is treated as the strongest link. As an example, a burial record of a child may well contain the names of the child's father and mother as well as the name of the child itself. If it is linked to a baptism record which also carried the name of the father and mother, that link will possess two positive matches (in addition to the agreement in the names of the child itself). It would outscore a rival link from the burial to another baptism on which only the father was named.

Age is the next most stable characteristic in the information fields which make up a record. Indeed if age were always accurately known and recorded precisely it would be as invariant as names, or more exactly, stated age would bear an unchanging relationship to fixed dates, such as birth or marriage. If the matchscoring of names fails to produce a winner, therefore, age is considered next. The procedure parallels that with names. If two competing links each possess age information, the more accurate of the two is preferred; while if one possesses age information and the other does not, the former is preferred.[25]

After the name and age/date rounds of matchscoring a strongest link will often have been identified. Indeed unless the register contains very little information this will almost always be the case. However, it is clearly possible in principle that matters should still be unresolved. Two main options are now open, and may be selected according to the aims of the study. The first is to choose at random between the links which remain in competition because they have scored equal highest. The random selection can either be simple in the sense that each link remaining stands an equal chance of success, or a weighting system may be used in which the inherent likelihood of the links is reflected. For example, if there were only two links remaining and both were BAP–BUR links, a link in which the time interval between the two records is 96 years is less likely than one in which the interval is 6 months. The disadvantage of any departure from simple random scoring is, of course, that it involves building assumptions into the resolution of clusters which may introduce bias into the end result. If links of this type are flagged, however, they can always be excluded from tabulation at a later stage.

The second option is to make use of information about occupation and residence contained in the records. If the analysis of, say, occupa-

---

[25] It may be noted that during the primary linking stage at the beginning of the reconstitution program, a substantial age/date discrepancy between two records which would otherwise be linkable acts as a bar to linkage (just as a name mismatch in a field where a name match is not mandatory similarly acts as a bar to linkage, although in both the age/date field and the non-mandatory name fields absence of information is not a bar to linkage). Since this test is used at the primary linkage stage, stated ages are always tolerably accurate in linked record pairs.

tional mobility is a prime object of study it would clearly be inappropriate to use occupational information in matchscoring since this will entail giving preference to links without occupational change over those in which a change of occupation occurred. In a purely demographic study this would be a less cogent deterrent. Occupational matches are scored positively, mismatches negatively, while lack of information means a null score. The scoring of positive matches can be weighted by the relative rarity of the occupation within the population as a whole (peruke makers, for example, were much rarer than husbandmen).[26] If making use of information from the occupation fields still produces no matchscore winner, the competition may be extended to the residence field, before resorting finally to random selection. If this is done the system as a whole becomes a four-stage preferential system (name, age, occupation, residence) and the program jumps out at whatever stage a matchscore winner emerges. The winning link is flagged so that any combination of types of winning link can be specified at the tabulation stage. The overall frequency of links of different types is also counted at the tabulation stage. In a register of the quality of the best French examples, it is quite likely that the program would never need to go beyond the first stage (names) in resolving clusters.

The system sketched here seeks to maximize the probability that the life histories of the individuals whose records are present in a cluster will be correctly put together. More certain links are given preference over less certain and the cluster as a whole is slowly decomposed by the successive deletion of links which are incompatible with other and stronger links.

Other approaches are possible. For example, Skolnick describes in Chapter 5 a method of resolving clusters which seeks to preserve the maximum total score for a cluster as a whole. Since the size of the score is dependent not only on the strength of the links but also on their number, there is some danger that a solution which preserves a large number of relatively weak links will score more highly than a solution with fewer links but higher individual link scores. Since the entity being studied is the individual life and not a cluster (whose very existence reflects uncertainty about individual lives), there may be dangers in a strategy which attempts to preserve a maximum total score for clusters as a whole, but until more is known about the outcome of the two strategies by comparing their results on the same body of data it is premature to be dogmatic about their characteristics.

---

[26] Very serious occupational mismatches (e.g. clergyman/carpenter) are, of course, as mentioned earlier, a bar to linkage at the primary linkage stage.

It should be noted that simultaneous examination of all information fields can be so scored that it does not necessarily favour occupational and residential immobility. If the frequency with which there is agreement and disagreement in the several information fields has been tabulated for a sample of truly and falsely linked record pairs, this knowledge can be used to calculate for each link an overall score representing the probability that it is a true link. This method, which depends upon the calculation of likelihood ratios has been widely used, and it may be helpful to outline it briefly to make clear the contrast between this approach and the preferential scoring method just described. The following steps are usually taken.[27] The first four are preliminary operations and serve as a basis for the matching operations (stages 5 and 6).

1   A sample of records is drawn from two files and pairs of records are matched visually to determine whether they constitute true or false links.

2   For each information field in turn (e.g. occupation, age) the frequencies of agreements and disagreements are tabulated for true and false links.

3   From these frequencies two ratios are calculated; the ratio of true links to false links in cases where the records agree, and a similar ratio in cases where the records disagree.

4   These ratios, or odds, are converted to convenient scores by expressing the odds as a logarithm to the base 2.

5   All possible record pairs are matched and an appropriate score is obtained for each information field, depending on whether the records agree or disagree in the field. The overall odds that the record pair constitutes a true or false link are calculated by adding together the logarithm scores obtained separately for each item of information.

6   Some score is selected as a cut off point. Any scores higher than this are taken to imply a true potential link. If more than one score qualifies the higher score may be preferred.

[27] This procedure was developed by the Atomic Energy of Canada Ltd., team and is described in several of their publications. The most useful accounts are in H. B. Newcombe, *et al.*, 'Automatic linkage of vital records', *Science* (1959,) 954–9, and H. B. Newcombe and J. M. Kennedy 'Making maximum use of the discriminating power of identifying information', *Communications of the Association for Computing Machinery* V, (1962) 563–6. A general statistical expression of this approach has been given by A. B. Sunter, 'A statistical approach to record linkage', in E. D. Acheson (ed.), *Record linkage in medicine*, Proceedings of the International Symposium Oxford, July 1967 (Edinburgh, 1968).

Essentially, therefore, this approach uses the likelihood ratios of true and false links in the sample files to derive a set of rules for discriminating between true and false links in the files of records at large. It thus adopts the classical approach to hypothesis testing, which seeks to minimize the level of one type of error for any given level of error of the other type. Providing, therefore, that the assumptions made about the method used are in fact justifiable, it should provide an efficient method of discriminating between potential record links. And indeed this scoring procedure appears to give excellent results with both modern and nineteenth century records.[28] But it assumes that the scores obtained for each item of information are independent. And this assumption is questionable since it is probable that the items of information on individual records do not occur in random combinations; for example, residence may be correlated with occupation and occupation with age. Although investigations of the amount of intercorrelation between different information fields in linked files of records have so far yielded negligible results,[29] this does not dispose of the problem of intercorrelation completely. Each score, whether for agreement or disagreement, is based on the relative frequencies of true and false links, determined by means of a preliminary visual linking of the sample record. The criteria used in deciding at this preliminary stage whether a potential link between two records is true or false have never been fully specified, but if they include taking into account the *number* of information fields on which the two records agree or disagree (for example disregarding a digit inversion in a date because the records agree on all other points), then it follows that the relative frequencies of true and false links in cases of agreement (and disagreement) of the different items will be positively intercorrelated. Thus summing the log odds scores will overstate the overall odds that a given potential link is true or false. Furthermore, the scale which the sum of the log odds represents will be isometric to the interval scale normally used to express odds only when the intercorrelation is zero.[30] However, providing the overall scores are based on the same

[28] In addition to the papers by Newcombe already cited, see H. B. Newcombe and P. O. W. Rhynas, 'Family linkage of population records' in *The use of vital and health statistics for genetic and radiation studies*, U.N. publication, Sales No. 61, XVII, i (1962), 135–54. Also I. Winchester, 'The linkage of historical records by man and computer: techniques and problems', *Journal of Interdisciplinary History*, I (1970), 107–24, esp. 123.

[29] Winchester, *Journal of Interdisciplinary History*, (1970), 122; and Newcombe and Kennedy *Communications of the Association for Computing Machinery* (1962), 563–4.

[30] If the degree of intercorrelation varies between different items of information, changes in the number of information fields considered will produce overall scores which comprise different scales. It then becomes difficult to use changes in the distribution of the overall scores as a measure of the extra degree of 'discrimination' afforded by an additional item of information (as in Newcombe, *Science* (1959), 957).

information fields, they will comprise an ordinal scale, and can still be used meaningfully to eliminate potential links which score less than some cut-off point on the scale, and to prefer higher-scoring links.

In certain circumstances therefore the likelihood ratio approach may produce results which are difficult to evaluate[31] and it suffers from the disadvantage that resources have to be expended on a preliminary visual linking of a sample set of records in order to identify which potential links are true and which are false, an unnecessary step if a preferential scoring system is used.

In the preferential scoring system which we have adopted it is possible to use a very simple scoring system in the first stage (names) in which positive agreement in the various name fields is additive and each such agreement scores equally with any other. However, the system may be refined to give greater discrimination by weighting the score for each accordant name pair in two records in such a way that the score reflects the probability that the link occurred by chance. Thus, there is a higher probability of this happening with John than with Zachariah, and a link with the latter name pair would score higher than one with the former. For example, in the case of a baptism record in which both the maternal and paternal grandfathers were mentioned and were called Zachariah and John, a BAP–MAR [parents] link to a marriage record which named Zachariah but not John would be preferred to one which named John but not Zachariah, *ceteris paribus*. The second stage (age/date) operates on the basis that the least discrepancy wins. The third stage (occupation) is scored in the same way as the refined version of the name scoring. Where data in other information fields are suitable for similar treatment, and on the assumption that the information fields so analysed are independent of each other, it is possible to combine the probabilities obtained to derive for any combination of information items from these fields an overall probability of drawing at random a record which matches another in respect of these items.[32]

[31] It is not clear whether the results of the most fully reported investigation (that of the Atomic Energy of Canada Ltd) in fact support the likelihood ratio approach, for the scores of four out of the six information fields originally used (initials and birthplaces of husband and wife) were based on simple frequencies and not on a true/false link likelihood ratio. Newcombe *Science* (1959), 956.

[32] In English parish registers the only field, other than occupation, which might be treated in this way is residence but it is difficult in many areas to frame accurate equivalence rules for place names (chiefly because of the bewildering variety of hamlet and farm names within the parish or just outside it which may be used in the register). We have not attempted to treat residence in this way. In principle, however, it would be valuable to

THE GENERAL SIGNIFICANCE OF NOMINAL RECORD LINKAGE USING HISTORICAL MATERIALS

It is perhaps a fair generalization that the greater the extent of the articulated information about an individual or a family, whether present in some original record or derived by record linkage, the greater the ease and certainty with which further information may be added, and once added, used to good effect. For example, when family reconstitution has assembled much information about some families in a parish and some information about most, other sources may be used much more effectively than could otherwise be the case, as when a knowledge of the number and age of the children helps to make Poor Law transfer payments easier to interpret, or throws light on the arrangements for property transfer made in a will.

---

compare the results of the likelihood ratio method with a method consisting in the following three preliminary and two matching steps.

1   A frequency count of the particular instances of each item of information is derived in a pre-pass.
2   The probability of drawing a record at random with an information field (k) containing a particular item of information (i) is calculated as

$$p = \frac{n_{(k, i)}}{n_{(k, \text{stated})}}$$

3   The scores for agreement or disagreement between two records on a particular item of information are calculated as

Agreement: $\log_2 \frac{1}{p}$

Disagreement: $-\log_2 \frac{1}{(1 - p)}$

If the information field is empty in either record, there is no evidence either in favour of or against a link, and zero is scored.

4   For each record pair, the scores for agreement or disagreement for each information field are calculated, and an overall score is obtained by summing the individual log scores.
5   Where there are competing links, the link with the highest score may be preferred. In appropriate circumstances a minimum cut-off score may be used just as with the likelihood ratio method.

Both the likelihood ratio method and this method based on frequency counts depend upon there being few empty information fields in the bulk of the records. If the information content of the records is poor, there is little point in setting up elaborate procedures to discriminate between competing links. This is one reason for adopting the preferential scoring system for family reconstitution using English parish registers. All record linking operations may share the same goals, but the best strategy for achieving these goals will depend to a large extent on the limitations of the records and the purposes for which the particular study was undertaken.

The whole set of record linkage operations which has just been described in outline is intended to operate within a single record context, that of the parish registers. Many of the detailed tests, which occupy much of the total coding, relate to rare conditions found only in English parish registers (or sometimes in vital registration more generally).[33] We have written very little about tests of this type but have sought instead to concentrate on questions which are likely to arise when using nominal record linkage methods for many types of historical source material, and not simply in computerizing family reconstitution. In particular there will almost always be problems, when using nominal record linkage methods in any such data context, in specifying the conventional conditions which must be met before two records are regarded as referring to the same individual. The solution adopted may take the form of a single criterion or set of criteria which must be met before a link is formed. Alternatively, it may mean the formation of links of different types, as in the present essay where three strategies can each produce a link (no competition with any other link; matchscore preference on a probability basis; and random allocation). Some of the algorithms developed in the context of family reconstitution will probably prove applicable in other contexts. They are written as subroutines to be called when the current data have been treated in a way appropriate to their particular nature.

Intercensal nominal record linkage, or linkage between census books and directories, for instance, produce problems cognate with those discussed in this essay, especially in cases where an individual or family has moved from one house to another in the same census district between the taking of the earlier and the later census (where a family remains at the same address at two successive censuses, there are so many information fields whose congruence can be tested that there is unlikely to be any ambiguity). Here, too, the underlying issue is the same. There are a number of information fields which must agree before any link can be made, but there may be several possible links which meet minimal requirements, only one of which can ultimately be confirmed. And, as in a parish register context, it may be that if entries which may relate to the same individual occur in several successive censuses the complexity of the possible links will increase notably (with analogues to the states of multiplicity, in-

---

[33] For example, a baptism record may occasionally be so phrased as to make it clear that the father died before his child was born. This pinpoints the period within which the father must have died and modifies the linkage algorithm which forms links between the husband of the marriage and appropriate burial records.

compatibility and backtracks found in nominal record linkage based on parish registers).

Nor does the basic issue change when nominal records drawn from vital records and census lists are to be merged to cover the life histories of individuals and families and the structure of their households and kinship patterns.[34] Once more certain minimal criteria must be met before any link can be formed between two records, but many more links may initially be brought into being than are mutually compatible. To make the best of this cluster of linkages a suitable algorithm to remove incompatibilities must be employed, and it is convenient to frame the algorithm so that it produces optimal solutions both when the information is excellent and when there is little to go on. Where possible there appears normally to be great advantage in postponing final decisions about the deletion of links to the last feasible moment so that the most can be made of the information in the full cluster. This is not possible when decisions are made *ad hoc* as the links are built up.

Refinements which mean distinguishing between links of different degrees of probability would not be worth pursuing if record keeping had normally been so full and exact that they would be useful in only a tiny minority of cases. But historical records frequently fall well short of this standard, and this must be the justification for a more complex strategy. It is possible to test the reliability of the results produced in this way by a simple procedure. If a record source known to be of high quality were used in conjunction with a program which allowed both 'high' and 'low' quality links to form freely in its early stages, but used the available information efficiently to prefer the former to the latter in case of conflict later on, the results could be compared with the results obtained from the same material, but with certain categories of information systematically suppressed. For example, one might run a program of the type described in this essay on a parish register of high quality, like Crulai, procure a print-out of reconstituted families using the information in the register to the full, but then suppress from the file (or from consideration by the record linkage program) all information about, say, age, and so discover how similar the results would be, and how frequently decisions about linkage in the second case were made only after the match-

---

[34] This type of merge is peculiarly valuable because it reveals things which cannot be gleaned from either source taken separately. When marriage records are used in conjunction with census records, for example, residence patterns of affinal kin can be traced, which is not possible when census records alone are used, while, on the other hand, household composition is immediately clear from census records though it cannot be reconstructed from a vital register.

scoring of alternatives. Congruence in results would provide a reasonable basis for the hope that relatively poor sources could be used to advantage given a program which is adapted to the difficulties of more haphazard and arbitrary record keeping.

APPENDIX ON NAME SPELLING

Variation in the spelling of names is problematical not only for historians but also for organizations such as hospitals and airlines which need to link personal records. Considerable research effort has therefore been put into devising efficient computer methods for eliminating spelling variations in names.[35] Inconsistencies in spelling arise either because of errors in writing (for example through a transposition of characters), or because of different character representations of phonetic sounds. The solutions usually adopted involve the elimination of selected characters, notably vowels and double consonants, often coupled with a truncation of the remaining characters. Scholars working in the field of record linkage have almost universally adopted the most phonetically orientated of the procedures for standardized spelling—the Russell Soundex code. In its original form the Soundex code retains the initial letter and replaces the remaining characters by three numerals representing the first three consonants encountered. These numbers are chosen so that the same numeral replaces consonants which are similar phonetically (e.g. B, P, F, and V are all coded 1).[36] Although the Soundex transformation brings together under the same code a number of variant spellings, it is not a notably efficient method of eliminating spelling inconsistencies even in modern conditions. In two recent North American studies, for example, the Soundex code eliminated only about two-thirds of surname spelling inconsistencies.[37] Spelling variation was far greater in the past, and Soundex is even less successful at overcoming it. For example, only a little over one half of spelling inconsistencies were eliminated by it in two files of mid-nineteenth century Canadian records.[38] Various modifications to the Soundex code have been

---

[35] The various approaches are reviewed in C. P. Bourne and D. E. Ford *Journal of the Association for Computing Machinery*, 8 (1961), 538–51.

[36] Full rules for Soundex are quoted in Winchester, *Journal of Interdisciplinary History* (1970), 115.

[37] Newcombe, *Science* (1959), 957; and D. M. Nitzberg, 'Results of research into the methodology of record linkage', in Acheson (ed.) *Record Linkage*, 193.

[38] The percentage of discrepant surnames in truly linked record pairs in Hamilton, Ontario (1851–2) was 25%. Winchester, *Journal of Interdisciplinary History* (1970), 116.

proposed, notably the numerical coding of the initial letter and special treatment of aberrant character strings (such as Mac).[39] Special procedures of this kind, which are geared to the specific orthographic vagaries of the records are much more effective than a standard phonetic code. For example, in the Hamilton study while Soundex alone overcame only 56 per cent of discrepant spellings, Soundex together with special pre-treatment of character strings eliminated 80 per cent of the discrepancies.[40] Special procedures are even more necessary in the case of forenames to overcome the problem of diminutives which differ phonetically from the full form of the name.

Any scheme for overcoming spelling variations can be in error in two ways. Firstly it can fail to collate genuinely variant spellings. This is the more serious failing of the two, because the omitted record will subsequently not even be considered for linking to records in the correct name set. But a standardizing scheme can also fall into error by grouping together names which are genuinely different. This both raises the cost of record linkage, by introducing a number of needless inter-record comparisons, and more seriously, leads to a risk of making spurious links. If the records consistently contain a number of additional items of information (such as age, sex, occupation, residence), this risk becomes very low, but in many historical situations this information is lacking and the danger of making spurious links is a real one. If, in addition, the record linking forms part of a wider decision process, in which subsequent links between records depend upon the presence or absence of earlier links, then clearly it is essential to reduce *both* kinds of surname grouping error to the minimum.

It is clear even from a casual inspection of early English parish registers that none of the fully automatic procedures for standardizing the spelling of names, such as Soundex, is capable of grouping genuinely variant spelling in the context of the erratic orthography of the sixteenth and seventeenth centuries. We have, however, confirmed this judgement by subjecting the forenames entered in the first 100 years of the Colyton register (1538–1640) to standardization by the most successful of the Soundex variants.[41] An independent study identified 986 spellings comprising 244 different names. Soundex both failed to assign 14 per cent of the *spellings* to the

[39] W. Phillips, 'Record linkage for a chronic disease register', in Acheson (ed.), *Record Linkage*, 132–5; A. Smith, 'Preservation of confidence at the central level', in Acheson (ed.) *Record Linkage*, 340–2; Winchester, *Journal of Interdisciplinary History* (1970), 116–17.
[40] Winchester, *Journal of Interdisciplinary History* (1970), 117.
[41] This variant, known as SINGS (Soundex Initial Numericized, Granick Smith), also groups the initial letter phonetically. A. Smith in Acheson (ed.), *Record linkage*, 342.

appropriate name, and erroneously conflated about one third (35 per cent) of the *names*. The principle causes of failure with Soundex were its inability to suppress silent consonants (for example, 'd' in Bridget), leading to variant spellings being missed, and its gross grouping of consonants (for example the letters c, g, j, k, q, s, x, z are treated as equivalent), which produced the massive conflation of genuinely different names. Error rates as high as this, which are likely to occur in any standard system when applied to early spelling practice, are unacceptable, and lead to the conclusion that fully automatic standardization of name spellings in general, and Soundex in particular, must be abandoned. Since picking out variant spellings from an alphabetical list by eye is a tedious and fallible operation, it seems sensible to use the computer to produce preliminary groupings which can then be checked by eye. And since it is easier to identify conflations of separate names than dispersed spellings of the same name, this preliminary standardization should over- rather than under-group the names.

A program has therefore been written which adds to each record a standardized version of the spelling of a name, and prints out an alphabetically sorted list of the standardized names together with the corresponding original spellings.[42] The program considers each letter of a name in turn, taking into account its position in the word and the letters which precede and follow it, and it is therefore a simple matter to change the program to suit different spelling conventions. The program has been tested on the file of forenames from the first 100 years of the Colyton register. It was no better than Soundex at overcoming the more outrageous sixteenth century spelling variations; as with Soundex 14 per cent of the 986 spellings failed to be assigned to the correct names. However, whereas Soundex tended to group these variants erroneously with other names, the program usually left them isolated, and quite near to the correct name in the alphabetical list so that they were easy to find. The main superiority of the program over Soundex lay in its greater discrimination between genuinely different names, for while Soundex conflated 35 per cent of the names, the program conflated 21 per cent.

The program therefore performs a reasonable preliminary spelling standardization, and it does so quickly and at a modest cost.[43] Ultimately it is still necessary, however, to use human judgement to

---

[42] The program is written in PL360 and when compiled can be used on any IBM 360 or 370 machine.

[43] It handles 46,000 (IBM 370) characters per second of Central Processing Unit time. At rates prevailing in English universities this is equivalent to £0·25 for 10,000 personal names, at an average of 13 characters to the name.

decide whether different spellings are variants of the same name, or represent different names. But the use of standardized names, expressed in letters rather than numbers and sorted into alphabetical order, makes this a far more pleasant and secure task than when working with the original spellings. In addition, the standardizing program performs over two-thirds of the work and the alterations which need to be made (for example, distinguishing between BARON and BROWN conflated under BRN) can easily be implemented by a further correction program.

Family reconstitution of early parish register entries poses some exceptionally severe problems, but there may well be other situations in which either the extreme variability of the spelling of historical records, or the need to avoid errors in dividing the file into record comparison sets, makes it sensible to settle for less than a fully automatic standardization of names.

Mark Skolnick

5 The resolution of ambiguities in record linkage*

INTRODUCTION

Historians and demographers have been hampered in the study of the demographic transition which accompanied the industrial revolution by the limitations inherent in census materials. Censuses are not always available, and in any case individual vital histories cannot be derived from them. Yet only by reconstructing the genealogies of individuals can an accurate picture of some aspects of population structure be obtained. To reconstruct genealogies we need to know the date and location of each person's birth, death, and marriage. In addition, we must identify his parents and children. Correlation between one event, say the death of a person, and other events, such as migration of his children, death of a spouse, or inheritance of property, can then be examined using information which refers to individuals rather than the entire population.

Reconstruction of genealogies is also of interest to the population geneticist. He is interested in the correlation between fertility patterns of consanguins, levels of consanguinity and inbreeding, migration patterns, and the demographic parameters which affect the distribu-

* The author wishes to thank Professors L. L. Cavalli-Sforza and A. Moroni for their collaboration and for their permission to refer to the Parma Valley data. He also wishes to thank Dr A. W. F. Edwards for advice on the use of likelihoods; Dr B. Buchanan, Mr L. Masinter and Mr S. Stavitsky for discussion about the use of heuristic searches; Mr R. Kelley, Dr C. Cannings, and Dr N. Yasuda for assistance in deriving equations for the total number of solutions; Mr D. Barbieri for assistance with the IBM 360/44 at the University of Pavia; and Mrs E. Zanardi-Carraro for preparing the figures and for technical assistance.

This chapter is based on work supported in part by a grant from the Consiglio Nazionale delle Ricerche to the University of Pavia under the Stanford-Pavia Exchange Program, and also by a grant from the Atomic Energy Commission, AT (30-1)-2280 to support computing facilities.

tion of children ever born. His interest in measuring the nature of the gene flow in a population is similar to the historian's interest, in that they both depend on a detailed reconstitution of the population and the subsequent analysis of social phenomena which determine movement, survival, and reproductive patterns.

We have developed a general method for linking records drawn from more than one source. The records must contain sufficient nominal information to identify individuals. For example, the baptism, burial, and marriage registers kept by most Christian churches can provide full genealogical information. In addition, nominal household censuses taken by parish priests, civil records of a similar nature, newspapers, actuarial records, and other sources of nominal information may be used in record linking. Physical characteristics such as height, weight, finger prints, and other such identifiers found in hospital and judicial records may also be used. Such additional sources, while of secondary importance genealogically, will provide other valuable information about individuals in the population being studied. Personal genealogies are created by linking birth, burial, and marriage records found in baptism, burial, and marriage parish registers, and can then be extended when links are found to an individual's spouse, parents, and children. If all the links are unambiguous, the individual's records form a genealogical graph with links to his spouse, parents, and children.

Unfortunately records may sometimes be linkable to more than one individual in the population. In these cases we have tried to evaluate the likelihood that the information pertains to each of the individuals in the population, and resolve the ambiguities by finding the Maximum Likelihood linkage.[1]

The proposed method of linking first finds all possible links of each type; birth–death, birth–marriage, marriage–marriage, marriage–death, husband–wife, father–child, and mother–child. Where there are no ambiguities, records are linked. In cases where there are ambiguities to be resolved, all of the possible links involved should be considered together; however they may be considered independently of other links. In addition likelihoods may be assigned to a number of links as a unit where the likelihood of one link is dependent on the existence of other links. Ideally, all of the ambiguities in a sub-group should be resolved simultaneously to produce the solution which is most likely to be correct. As this ideal cannot always be met for lack of computer time and space, a part of the method presented is a set

[1] A complete discussion of likelihood is given by A. W. F. Edwards, *Likelihood* (Cambridge University Press, 1972).

of rules which allow one to deviate from this principle with a minimum chance of introducing error. As many types of ambiguity exist, we offer several examples to illustrate how the proposed methods function in different situations.

The optimum strategy in resolving ambiguities will depend upon the object in view. For example, it may be important to avoid making false links. In such a case, with a high premium on certainty or near certainty, where an ambiguity was present every effort would be made to try to ensure that the most certain links were always retained. The result would be a smaller number of nearly certain links. This method might be used by a historian assembling information relating to a famous personage, or by a lawyer presenting evidence in court where uncertain evidence is not admissible. It would also be used by a geneticist who was reconstructing the pedigrees of a couple for genetic counselling, where many missing branches in the pedigree are preferable to a more complete pedigree with some incorrect branches. In such cases, the reconstruction of each pedigree is an independent event.

A second method may be more appropriate where the goal is the reconstitution of the population of an area as fully as possible. In this endeavour one is less concerned with occasional individual errors, than with systematic biases introduced in linking. In this case, not linking a baptism record to a burial record is equivalent to saying that two people existed, one who was born in the area and later emigrated, and a second who immigrated and died in the area of study. Therefore, it is important to test that the total number of links made of each type, e.g. birth–death, death–marriage is equal to the estimated true number of links of each type, and that incorrect links are unbiased. In this way, the population will be reconstituted with as little bias as possible overall. The disadvantage of creating a greater number of uncertain links by this method is offset by not introducing a bias which would be present if only records relating to the select subset of individuals about whom information is certain were linked. We believe that errors introduced by uncertainty will affect the analysis less than the biases introduced by selective linking and that it is best to estimate the resulting migration matrix, family size distribution, life tables and other demographic parameters in this way. In any case, by attaching a likelihood coefficient to each link, analysis can be performed in several ways, and the results compared. The second method may even give more accurate results by rejecting the apparent best link in some cases. Each link, rather than being considered singly is determined by examining alternate links, and it may be that by accepting a link which is a best fit for one record, one is forced to make a number of poorer fits in several other records, which casts doubt on the apparent best link.

RECORD LINKING BY COMPUTER

Those who have reconstructed genealogies by hand are aware of the complexity of the decision-making process and may be sceptical of the possibility of performing such a complicated procedure mechanically. The computer has no special power which men do not have, but the computer does have some characteristics which make it an efficient tool for record linking. Because the data are recorded electronically, they can be manipulated, transcribed, and compared at electronic speed. The reams of paper and years of human labour consumed performing the same operations by hand are saved. Barring a system failure, the computer is a slave to the programmed algorithm. This makes casual error virtually impossible. The speed of the computer makes it possible to evaluate many alternate solutions and select the best, an operation which one would be reluctant to perform manually.

The sceptic might argue that the computer lacks the ability to make intuitive judgement used in linking records, but we believe that the algorithms used are preferable to the use of intuition and substitute for it a quantitative investigation of a larger solution space. The illusive biases and inconsistencies of reconstitution by hand will become quantified and consistent, and hopefully with experience they will be eliminated. However, the methods proposed are still being developed, and will undoubtedly be modified with experience.

PARISH REGISTERS

The method to be presented is a solution of a specific problem, that of forming genealogies from parish registers of baptisms, deaths, and marriages. These are the records which are most useful for reconstituting the population of a particular area, although other nominal registers could be used. A fourth church record, the *stati d'anime* (state of souls), a type of household census, is used to control the accuracy of the reconstitution obtained. The following brief description of the history of parish registers and their contents in various countries is intended to familiarize the reader with the data under consideration.

The earliest Italian parish registers are to be found in Siena (1379),

Pisa (1457), Parma (1459) and Piacenza (1466).[2] Some city states recognized these church records and gave civic value to the certificates issued by the church. Others established parallel civic records. Systematic registration of baptisms, burials and marriages in Catholic parishes of many countries began with the Council of Trent (1542–63) which ordered parish priests to keep all three registers. But the practice of keeping them began slowly and irregularly. Often baptism registers were initiated before burial and marriage registers. Unfortunately, in some parishes individual registers have been lost or destroyed creating gaps in the continuity of registration.[3]

There are slight variations in the data recorded which affect the exact strategy adopted in record linking. The Catholic registers appear to have age of death more frequently than Protestant registers. They also contain more complete nominal information describing the mother and father of the person, especially during the seventeenth and eighteenth centuries. The Spanish registers, and the registers of Central and South American countries under Spanish dominion, followed the custom of attaching the mother's surname to the surname of each person mentioned in the record. Thus, nominal identification becomes much more positive, since where the data is recorded completely the grandparents are partially identified, and the possibility for ambiguity is almost non-existent.

The problems of record linking will also depend on the size of the parishes, the amount of migration, and the detectability of migration in the area under study. In cities births and deaths are more likely to occur in different parishes. In areas where the parishes are large, record linkage is extremely difficult, as movements within the parish cannot be detected. On the other hand, in a genetic isolate where there is little immigration there tends to be a build up of some surnames, and their power as identifiers decreases. A further complication is the history of fission and fusion of parishes.

In Catholic countries women are recorded in burial registers with their maiden name. In other countries they may be recorded with their married surname, which greatly increases uncertainty in linking because baptism and burial records can be linked only through marriage records.

[2] A. Moroni, personal communication.
[3] M. H. Skolnick, A. Moroni, C. Cannings, and L. L. Cavalli-Sforza, 'The reconstruction of genealogies from parish books', in F. R. Hodson, D. G. Kendall and P. Tautu (eds.), *Mathematics in the Archaeological and Historical Sciences* (Edinburgh University Press, 1971), 319–34.

PARISH REGISTERS IN THE DIOCESE
OF PARMA

The method presented has been designed to deal with problems in linking records from the parish registers of three communes of the diocese of Parma: Monchio, Palanzano, and Corniglio. Together they form an isolated mountain valley in the upper part of the Parma river valley in northern Italy. The area is being studied genetically[4] because of the availability of many sources of information, and because the valley itself is a genetic isolate, a rural, hilly area bounded by mountains on three sides, and into which there was little immigration. Therefore, most marriages are between people born in the valley.[5] In addition, the parishes are quite small. With 40 parishes and a population of about 10,000 the mean population per parish is around 250. As the villages of birth and residence are included in the parish registers, it is often possible to pinpoint residence to a cluster of houses. This detail is important, as it allows one to follow internal migration very closely. However, the division of the area into small parishes, useful for migration studies, causes a complication in the early period. Since books started at different times in different parishes, there is much missing information in the early period, and genealogies which are spread among several neighbouring parishes are likely to be incomplete. In Parma approximately one third of baptism and marriage registers start during the sixteenth century, but only a twentieth of the burial registers begin this early. The *stati d'anime* or household censuses were taken sporadically and are first found in the sixteenth century in some parishes.[6] These village censuses give an accurate picture of who was living in each household at a given point in time. They provide a valuable check upon the accuracy of the links made as the reconstituted families can be compared with the census families. The two sources produce families which should differ only to the extent that children tended to migrate away from the parents' households, but since migration usually accompanied marriage, this offers further possibilities of checking results, rather than weakening the *stati d'anime* as a source of control.

Stati d'anime should theoretically have been taken every year by the parish priest. Actually, they were taken at greater intervals, the

---

[4] L. L. Cavalli-Sforza, 'Genetic drift in an Italian population', *Scientific American*, 22, no. 2 (1969), 20–37.

[5] L. L. Cavalli-Sforza, 'The distribution of migration distances; models and application to genetics', *Entretiens de Monaco en Sciences Humaines, Première Session, 24–29 May, 1962. Human Displacements* (1963), 139–58.

[6] A. Moroni, unpublished data.

frequency and completeness of the census varying widely from priest to priest. Some include age and relation to head of household; others only the name of each member of the household. These censuses also provide the data for a sociological investigation of household composition during the past several hundred years, showing for example, to what extent relatives and servants lived with families. Linked records combined with information on patterns of inheritance, especially in the case where only one son inherited his father's property while his brothers made their own way in life, should provide information on the variation of fertility among siblings. This and other factors which lead to the variation of fertility are of great genetic and sociological importance.

In the upper Parma valley very few parishes have continuous registration from the sixteenth century. Continuity is highly desirable, but is not always necessary. It is rather the unfortunate combination of missing books which makes reconstitution impossible. Although the reconstitution is weakened by missing data, the presence of baptism records alone is sufficient for continuing the genealogy in cases where the information on parents uniquely identify appropriate parental baptism records.[7] In other cases, however, reconstitution becomes impossible because of missing registers. Fortunately, marriage and baptism registers, the most important for genealogies, were usually the first to be kept. The date of death is not always vital for constructing genealogies, and if the baptism record is missing, it can sometimes be inferred from the age in marriage or burial records. Thus, unless all three records are missing, there is still some possibility of reconstitution.

The completeness of the data in each register varies. Often the surname of the mother is absent. In these cases offspring must be linked to the father, and the mother linked to the children only through the marriage record of the father. Important optional data exists in some of the records: the approximate age of a person when he died, the age at marriage, the parish of birth on marriage records, the residence of new couples after marriage, and on all three types of record, an indication whether the parents were alive or dead. The legitimacy of a birth is also recorded. All such information is valuable in resolving ambiguities when linking parish records. As the third name is generally absent on death and marriage records it is of little use in linking. Second names are present frequently enough for them to be of significance.

[7] Skolnick *et al.*, *Mathematics in the Archaeological and Historical Sciences.*

THE ARTIFICIAL INTELLIGENCE APPROACH TO RECORD LINKING

Two statistical approaches can be used to link records. The method presented by Wrigley and Schofield attempts to find the best links directly, and if after all the links of various types have been made, there is ambiguity, links incompatible with the strongest link are deleted until by iteration a solution is found.

The method which we present in this paper follows more closely the decision making techniques developed in artificial intelligence projects where computers are used in puzzle solving, chess playing, theorem proving, and similar examples of machine intelligence.[8] The artificial intelligence approach consists of building a family of related solutions, developing a method of keeping the family of reasonable solutions small, and selecting the best solution with minimum effort and maximum accuracy.

We shall describe how all reasonable links are found and evaluated. Where there is ambiguity, a tree of solutions is built which gives us all the reasonable solutions. For parts of the data sets which are of such high quality that reasonable alternative links will not be found, the method efficiently produces a correct linkage.

FINDING POTENTIAL LINKS

Before explaining the intricacies of finding potential links we must define some terms. An entry in a parish register of baptisms, burials, or marriages, is called a record. Marriage records are double records, as there is one record of information for the husband and one for the wife.

There are two types of intra-generational links. Type I links are between two or more entries which refer to the same person. Type II links are those between husband and wife. This type of link is usually contained in marriage records, but if a couple moves out of the parish, evidence of their marriage can still be obtained indirectly from other records. For example, if only the burial records of a couple are found, we can assume that the couple immigrated after their marriage. Type III (father–child) and Type IV (mother–child) links are inter-generational links.

[8] N. S. Nilsson, *Problem solving in A.I.* (McGraw-Hill, 1971). G. W. Ernst and A. Newel, *GPS: A case study in generality and problem solving*, (Academic Press, New York, 1969). Ira Pohl, 'Bi-Directional and heuristic search in path problems', SLAC Report no. 104, Stanford University, May 1969, Stanford, California.

Baptism records are indicated by the letter B, burial records by the letter D, and marriage records by the letter M. These records may stand alone as nodes in the final genealogical graph, or they can be joined together to form one record containing all the information of the combined records.

B nodes would be found for all persons who were baptized in the area of study but whose burial and marriage were not recorded in the area of study. Similarly, M and D nodes represent those who migrated during their life time and who were not in the area when they were baptized. Before links under consideration have been evaluated, linked records are to be thought of as nodes joined by their links. Once Type I links are accepted, the records are united into a single node representing an individual. Thus, a possible link between a baptism node and a burial node is notated by B–D, and a confirmed link is represented by a single BD node. The nodes in the final genealogies are indicated by combinations of the above three letters; BM, BD, MD, and BMD. If a person has been married twice, there will be combinations such as BMMD, BMM, and MMD. The ten

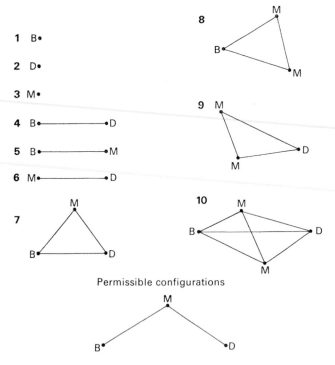

Permissible configurations

Example of an impermissible configuration

Figure 1

permissible configurations of Type I links are illustrated in Figure 1, and with the exception of cases where one person married three or more times, they represent the only configurations which are accepted as nodes by the computer program. Other configurations are not permissible, because they represent incomplete situations. In the example shown in Figure 1, the baptism record is linked to a marriage record, and the marriage record to a burial record, but the burial record is not linked to the baptism record. Either the additional link between the burial and baptism records must be made or one of the other links must be broken. To form links between the baptism, marriage and burial records of a person (Type I), the computer program takes a comparison group of records, consisting of all B, M, and D records with the same surname and first name, and examines each record of each type for possible linkage with each record of the other two types.[9] One might consider making the comparison groups smaller by breaking them down by date, but this is not possible as illustrated by Figure 2. A B record from 1800 might be linked to a D

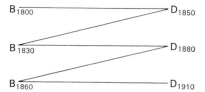

Figure 2

record from 1850 which might be linked to another B record from 1830 which is linked to a D record from 1880 and so on. Thus, the computer examines all data for linking during this phase if the surname and the first name are identical. It allows records with differing second and third names to be treated together. In this way a burial record for a John Smith which may refer to the death of John George Smith or John James Smith would be allowed to link to both records, if the dates, nominal identifiers, and other information show both links to be permissible. But no link is formed where there has been a name inversion involving the first name, or where there has been a mistake in the transcription of the first name. The surname and first forename are so essential to proper identification, that records which might link but which do not have matching surnames first names are separately treated when a sibling group is examined for consistency.

To find father–child and mother–child links, one must construct two other comparison sets, ordering the records by father's surname and first name, and by mother's surname and first name. By search-

[9] M. H. Skolnick, 'A computer program for linking records', *Historical Methods Newsletter*, vol. 4, no. 4 (1971) 114–25.

ing the parents in one group for all the children in the other group, all of the Type III and Type IV links can be found.

All possible marriage links are found by adding to the marriage links implied by each marriage record, the links between fathers and mothers indicated by B or D records. In this way marriages performed outside the parish are found.

FORMING CLUSTERS FOR THE RESOLUTION OF AMBIGUITIES

Trying to link the B, M, and D records of a person cannot always be done satisfactorily without linking the B, M, and D records of his children or his parents. This is usually true where the possibility of migration must be considered, and when one is seeking consistency in the migratory pattern of the family. Linking burial records to parents may exclude births after the parent's death, or information stating a parent as deceased on a potential child's marriage or burial record may be in conflict with a B–D link for the parent. For this reason it is important to look for all links before resolving ambiguities. In some instances the parent–child link is unambiguous, and is important in determining the intragenerational links. In other cases, the intragenerational links are unambiguous and are necessary to determine the parent–child links. With much missing data there may be both intra- and inter-generational ambiguities, and it will be important for these to be resolved simultaneously and in a consistent fashion. After all possible links are found, a cluster of these links is formed consisting of all links which are tied together by ambiguity. Each cluster must be resolved as a unit and the potential links are stored together. For records which form no links, special techniques must be used to test for spelling errors or other errors which would cause them not to link.

FORMATION OF LIKELIHOODS

The use of probabilities in distinguishing between random association and true association was suggested as early as 1718 by de Moivre in *Doctrine of Chances*.[10] He states,

> Further, the same Arguments which explode the Notion of Luck, may, on the other side, be useful in some Cases to establish a due

[10] Edwards, *Likelihood*, p. x.

comparison between Chance and Design: We may imagine Chance and Design to be, as it were, in Competition with each other, for the production of some sorts of Events, and may calculate what Probability there is, that those Events should be rather owing to one than to the other.

The frequencies of the nominal identifiers in the records to be linked forms the basis of the likelihoods. If one has the distribution of each forename and surname by parish, by time period and by type of record, one can calculate the probability that a link between two records will occur by chance. Thus, if a record has much missing data, and the only data which is compatible consists of common names, the probability of a match, made at random, being compatible by name is quite large. If there are many identifiers, and some of them are rare names, the probability of a compatible match occurring by chance is quite low, and can be estimated.

As each nominal identifier can be considered independently, the probability of a fortuitous association, P, is the product of the squares of the probabilities of each matching nominal identifier, thus:

$$P = \prod_{k=1}^{n} f_k^2 \qquad (1)$$

where the f_k are the frequencies of the k matching nominal identifiers. For the probability of two records, chosen at random, one from each parish, matching for the kth identifier is f_k^2, and for all k identifiers is therefore P. Note that we do not use the 'matching distributions' of statistical theory because we are content to use the large population approximations.

The probability of a random association can be converted into a likelihood of a link being correct by using the following formula:

$$L = \frac{\alpha}{P}. \qquad (2)$$

where α is the probability of finding the link in the area of study. It is 1 if we confidently expect a link to some record in the area of study on the basis of having found complete life histories for siblings or other relatives. If the parish is near the boundary of the study area, and the possibility of migration increases, α decreases. If there is a parish register missing which might contain the record we are seeking, then α also decreases. Thus, the above likelihood also encompasses the probability of emigration or missing data. The calculation of α may be difficult in some cases, but since α will usually be the same or of similar magnitude for two competing links, its imprecision is not of major significance. We offer a formula for the calculation of α which would be appropriate if migration were inversely proportional to the square of the distance between the places involved and proportional to their population sizes, though others might be suggested:

$$\alpha_j = \frac{\sum_{i=1}^{n} \frac{P_i}{d_{ij}^2} \cdot K}{\sum_{i=1}^{n} \frac{P_i}{d_{ij}^2}} \tag{3}$$

where $d_{ii} = 1$, P_i is an estimate of the population of the ith parish, d_{ij} the distance between i and j, and K a value which $= 1$ if data are available and o if data are missing or not considered in the study. The i parishes should include all parishes which are close enough or large enough to affect the calculation of α.

The use of name frequencies may be a crucial factor in linking. Although the number of matches gives an indication of the quality of a link, the rarity of each nominal identifier is also an important factor.

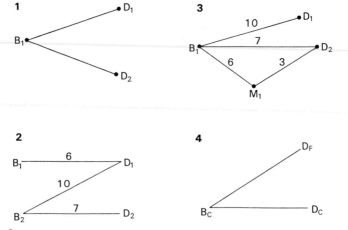

Figure 3

Case 1 of Figure 3 illustrates the importance that frequency may have in resolving ambiguity. In this case, one B record can link to two D records. Assume that the nominal information is the principal method of selecting a link. We might find records such as:

Baptism of James John Smith son of John George and Mary Jane
   Jones (B_1)
Burial of James Smith son of John and Mary Jane Jones (D_1)
Burial of James John Smith son of John George and Mary (D_2)

In each B–D link there are six matches, the distinction being an
additional match with the mother's surname and second name in one
record and a match with the child's and the father's second name in
the other. Clearly, the frequency of these four names holds the key to
deciding which record to select. If one of them were rare, it would be
less likely for there to be a random association, and the link with the
rare name match should be selected. Random associations of this
nature will occur more frequently in genetic isolates where the most
common surnames often represent over one third of the residents of
a parish.[11] With fewer nominal identifiers present in the record, the
probability of a random association increases. In addition names such
as Maria are so common that they offer almost no additional
identification.

AGE ERROR DISTRIBUTIONS FROM
LINKED RECORDS

Likelihoods are also computed from age error distributions which are
formed from records whose links are most certain. The criteria for
certainty would vary from one data set to another, but in general the
links which qualified as certain would be selected from unambiguous
links. Only those with high likelihoods, based on the name frequency
distribution, should be used. The following age error distributions
are calculated:

1   The difference between date of birth as estimated from the date
    of baptism and date of birth as calculated from the age of death
    and the date of death on burial records (for B–D links).
2   The difference between date of birth as estimated from the date
    of baptism and the date of birth as calculated from the age at
    marriage and the date of marriage on marriage records (for
    B–M links).
3   The difference between date of birth as estimated from the age at
    burial and the date of burial, and the age at marriage and the
    date of marriage (for D–M links).

[11] L. L. Cavalli-Sforza, A. Moroni, and M. H. Skolnick, unpublished data.

These distributions become important where the name matches are identical and age is present on the records. Where there is missing data and the date of birth cannot be estimated from death or marriage distributions, the inverse of the number of intervals in the distribution is used as the likelihood to keep scores unbiased for missing data.

COMPARING LIKELIHOOD SCORES

Cases 2 and 3 of Figure 3 illustrate two major problems in record linking. In both cases resolution of the cluster may involve rejection of the most likely individual link. The log likelihoods of each potential link have been included in the figure. In case 2, we have the choice between accepting a B_2–D_1 link and leaving B_1 and D_2 unlinked, or between accepting B_1–D_1 and B_2–D_2 links and rejecting the single highest scoring link. In case 3, the two most acceptable solutions are accepting the B_1–D_1 and M_1–D_2 links or accepting the B_1–M_1, B_1–D_2, M_1–D_2 links and leaving D_1 unlinked.

In both cases accepting the highest score for the cluster as a whole means rejecting the highest scoring link. According to likelihood theory, the log likelihoods are additive and we should accept the highest total score. While we are dissatisfied with having rejected the highest score, we would be even more dissatisfied with rejecting two scores whose total are even greater than the highest score. Until this type of ambiguity is isolated from the registers, and such cases checked by hand, the problem remains unresolved.

The second major problem illustrated by these cases, and discussed more fully later, is that the number of links in each solution varies, and the number of historical persons implied also varies. In case two, one solution implies one resident, one immigrant, and one emigrant, and the other solution implies two residents. Correct resolution of such cases is therefore extremely important if migration is to be accurately estimated from reconstructed genealogies.

Finally there is the problem that where a triangle of linked records exists, as with B_1–D_2–M_1 in case 3, the three links will score more heavily than alternative solutions not involving a triangle, and that the method therefore favours triangles and over-links. Theoretically, the scores are additive, if the links are independent, but there may be dependence in such triangles, and we have therefore decided to score them as a unit, considering them as a single link, whose score may be less than the sum of the log likelihoods of each link.

COMPATIBILITY MATRIX

Once the list of links has been divided into clusters and records which link unambiguously, and links in clusters have been scored, one is in a position to prepare the links for selection. The compatibility of links in each cluster must be determined, and this is done by constructing a compatibility matrix. Each link is checked for compatibility with each other link, and scored o if compatible, and 1 if incompatible. For example, $B_1 - D_1$ links are incompatible with all $B_1 D_i$ links, where D_i represents the other death records in a cluster. All links are compatible with all links outside the cluster by definition, but may be incompatible with at least one link within the cluster. The $B_i - M_j - D_k$ triangles are included in the set of links. They may both be incompatible with other links and may contain incompatibilities among their component links. In this case either all three or only one of these links must be accepted in order to avoid impermissible configurations. Similarly a triangle is created between the father–child, mother–child, and husband–wife links for all of the links in the list that will form these triangles. Such triangles are treated in the same way as $B_i - M_j - D_k$ triangles. These may have the sum of their scores altered, in a manner similar to the B–M–D triangles if a dependence relationship exists.

Other dependence relationships exist in the data, and the dependence of one link on the acceptance of another can be accounted for in the comparison matrix. Case 4 of Figure 3 shows a case where the death record of a potential father, D_F, is compatible with a potential child's birth record, but not its death record. This could happen if the death record of the child indicated that the father was dead, and the date of the death record of the father is later than that of the child. In this case $B_C - D_F$ and $B_C - D_C$ are incompatible, a fact which would not be known until both the Type I and Type III links have been made. The incompatibilities are simply identified by placing a 1 in the proper positions of the compatibility matrix, which allows one but not both links to be included in a solution.

One also wants to make sure that the migration patterns of families is reasonable. For example it is unlikely that spouses will die in distant parishes, unless these parishes are the parishes of birth, or of residence of parents or siblings. Thus, solutions with unusual, unexplainable migration patterns should be eliminated. Migration is a function of the inverse of the distance,[12] and it is reasonable to suppose that when a choice must be made between a link which

[12] Cavalli-Sforza, *Entretiens de Monaco*.

relates two records from distant parishes, and two records from the
same parish or neighbouring parishes, that the latter is preferable.
Where the choice is between two pairs of distant records, other information such as vital events of relatives determined by the already

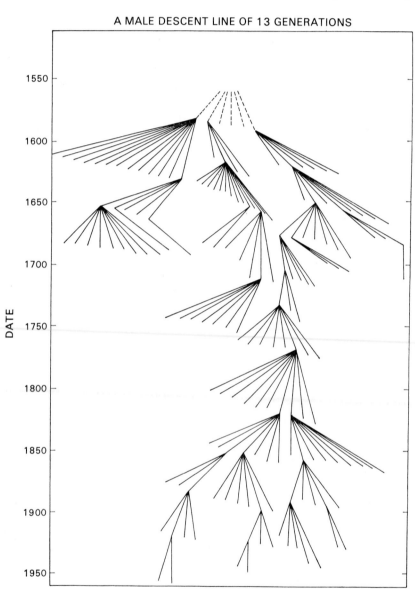

Figure 4

partially linked records and by male descent groups constructed on partially linked records may be used.

The genealogies ultimately obtained must be stored in a useful form. Male descent groups which extend across the area of study seem to be the most convenient choice. They consist of all members of the genealogy who have maintained the surname of the original ancestor. The complete genealogy is obtained by attaching all the descendants of married women in the male descent group.

Figure 4[13] gives an example of a male descent group of 13 generations from the parish of Bosco constructed from B records alone, accepting most probable fathers as parental nodes. The original ancestor, Peregrino Ferrari, is inferred from the information on the father in the baptism records of his five children. His date of baptism is uncertain, and is therefore indicated in the figure by converging dotted lines. The other lines in the figure are lines of descent from most probable fathers to children. By definition, all of the baptisms in the figure have the same surname.

When two sibling groups must be untangled and assigned to their parents, or when the preliminary male descent groups are ambiguous, it is indispensable to resort to a more complicated technique. As forenames are often passed to descendants, preliminary pedigrees and descent groups can be extremely helpful in resolving intergenerational links. Forenames are often passed from paternal grandfather to first sons. Forenames can also be passed to children from other relatives. A precise knowledge of the rules of forename inheritance, and when they are most often applied, is helpful in linking children to genealogies. Also, if the forenames are passed when the relative has recently died, additional information in linking death records is obtained. In such cases, the method proposed allows one to unite any group of links which may be dependent and score them as a unit. Thus the score of the unit would be decreased if the underlying migratory pattern were unlikely, and increased if it is thought that the unit as a whole is more likely than the sum of its parts. Similarly, patterns of name descent can cause the likelihood of the link unit to be increased or decreased if the unit upon examination has low probability based on rules of name inheritance.

To summarize, the likelihood of the links as computed in isolation can be altered as the more complete picture is recreated. When more than one reasonable solution exist, other factors not included in the calculation of likelihood can be used to decide which set of links is

---

[13] Figure 4 is reproduced from Hodson *et al.*, *Mathematics in the Archaeological and Historical Sciences.*

preferable. One might select a simple solution with a lesser score over a more complex solution with a slightly higher score.[14]

THE TOTAL NUMBER OF POSSIBLE SOLUTIONS[15]

In linking records, one might think that where there are ambiguities, one is trying to select between a limited number of possible solutions. The scale of the problem does not become evident until one has examined equations for the total number of solutions possible. Of these solutions, a large number may have very low likelihood, and may be discarded immediately, even though the most unlikely solution may be the correct one. The best we can do is find the most likely solution, that is the Maximum Likelihood Solution.

If one considers any two files, where the first file contains n records and the second file contains m records, and each record in the first file may link to each record in the second file, then the total number of possible solutions, $\Phi(m,n)$, is defined by the following equation:

$$\Phi(m,n) = \sum_{i=0}^{k} \binom{m}{i}\binom{n}{i} i! = \sum_{i=0}^{k} \frac{m!n!}{i!(m-i)!(n-i)!} \qquad (4)$$

where $k = \min(m,n)$. $f_{(n)}$ the number of sub-populations of size i of a population of n objects, is defined by

$$f_{(n)} = \binom{n}{i} = \frac{n!}{(n-i)!i!} \qquad (5)$$

and $g_{(n)}$, the number of ordered sub-populations is defined by

$$g_{(n)} = \binom{n}{i} i! = \frac{n!}{(n-i)!} \qquad (6)$$

One can see that equation (4) is the number of combinations of links to one file times the number of permutations of links to the other file summed over i, where i is the number of links. i takes on the values 0, 1, . . ., k, where k is the minimum of m and n, since the number of links between two files cannot exceed the number of elements in the smaller file.

[14] Edwards, *Likelihood*, chapter 10.
[15] The results of this section were derived in collaboration with R. Kelley and N. Yasuda and first appeared in, R. Kelley, M. H. Skolnick, and N. Yasuda, 'A combinatorial problem in linking historical records', *Historical Methods Newsletter* 6, no.1 (1972), 10–16.

The number of persons represented by each solution is $m + n - i$, that is the number of records minus the number of links.

Further,

$$\Phi(m,n) = \sum_{i=0}^{k} \binom{m}{i}\binom{n}{i}i! = k!\, L_k^{(|n-m|)}(-1) \tag{7}$$

where $k = \min(n,m)$, and L is the Laguerre polynomial defined by

$$L_n^{(\alpha)}(x) = \sum_{r=0}^{n} \binom{n+\alpha}{n-r}\frac{(-x)^r}{r!} \tag{8}$$

For three files, one finds the number of links possible between the third file and each solution for the two-file case, thus,

$$\sum_{i=0}^{k} \binom{m}{i}\binom{n}{i}i!\cdot\sum_{j=0}^{q}\binom{m+n-i}{j}\binom{p}{j}j! \tag{9}$$

where $k = \min(n,m)$, and $q = \min(n+m-i,p)$. Each new file requires the addition of another summation. Table 1 illustrates how

Table 1   The distribution of the number of persons in the solution space of $\Phi(m,n,p)$ where $m = n = p$

		Value of m				
		1	2	3	4	5
Number of persons	1	1				
	2	3	4			
	3	1	32	36		
	4		38	540	576	
	5		12	1,242	13,824	14,400
	6		1	882	50,668	504,000
	7			243	59,904	2,664,000
	8			27	30,024	4,608,000
	9			1	7,200	3,501,000
	10				856	1,350,360
	11				48	284,800
	12				1	33,800
	13					2,225
	14					75
	15					1
Total		5	87	2,971	163,121	12,962,661

rapidly the number of solutions builds up for the selected cases where $m = n = p$, and also shows the distribution of the number of historical persons represented in the solution space. The number of historical persons represented by a given solution is still the number of records minus the number of links, thus $m + n + p - i - j$ for the three-file case. Some of the j links are actually double links, as a j link which links to records already linked by an i link will have two actual links, one to a record in the m file, and one to a record in the n file, but in the above equation it is considered to be a single link to the combined m and n file.

The more than 12 million solutions for five B, five M, and five D records and the fact that the actual number of people who appear in the reconstitution varies, underlines the need for a meticulous solution.

THE PROBLEM SOLVER

A heuristic computer program, LINK, is being developed for the resolution of ambiguities in record linking. It is being constructed in a similar manner to the heuristic DENDRAL[16] computer program. Heuristic DENDRAL is a program which takes the mass spectrograph of an unknown organic compound and, by generating a tree of plausible compounds and comparing their theoretical spectra with the spectrograph of the unknown, the unknown can almost always be correctly determined. Failure to determine the correct compound reflects lack of expertise in the PREDICTOR part of the program, rather than a failure of the method. The success of the program lies not just in the ability to determine the unknown molecule correctly, but also in its ability to arrive at the solution rapidly. The program consists of three parts, a PLANNER, a STRUCTURE GENERATOR, and a PREDICTOR. An initial PLANNING phase defines constraints for the GENERATOR based on the data (spectrum) given. The GENERATOR takes an atom, and examines the possible ways in which chemical bonds or atoms can be selected as molecular centres. The n possible centres are stored at the first level of a tree structure, and each of them is in turn expanded by the addition of another atom in all possible ways.

[16] J. Lederberg, G. L. Sutherland, B. G. Buchanan and E. A. Feigenbaum, 'A heuristic program for solving a scientific inference problem. Summary of motivation and implementation', Stanford A. I. Memo AIM-104 (1969); J. Lederberg, G. L. Sutherland, B. G. Buchanan, E. A. Feigenbaum, A. V. Robertson, A. M. Duffield and Carl Diarassi, 'Applications of artificial intelligence for chemical inference. I. The number of possible organic compounds. Acyclic structure containing C, H, O and N', *Journal of the American Chemical Society*, 91 (21 May, 1969), 2973–6; B. G. Buchanan, G. L. Sutherland, E. A. Feigenbaum, 'Heuristic dendral: a program for generating explanatory hypotheses in organic chemistry', in B. Meltzer and D. Mikie (eds.), *Machine Intelligence IV* (Edinburgh, 1969), 209–54.

Each resulting structure is expanded in all possible ways, and so on until no more atoms remain to be attached. In this way a tree of molecular structures (solutions) is generated. Rather than generate all possible solutions, heuristics are used to prune improbable branches of the tree of solutions. The sooner pruning is done the more efficiently one arrives at the final solution. The speed of the program is therefore dependent mainly on the expertise of the programmer in deciding which branches to prune. If the test for pruning is time consuming, or has a low efficiency in finding prunable branches, then the program is inefficient.

LINK is a program for generating a set of solutions S, where the S_m solutions are all possible combinations of the n links and link units, L_i, such that if L_a and L_b are in S_e, L_a is compatible with L_b. The value of S is $f(S) = \sum_{i=1}^{n} L_i I_i$ (the predictor functions) where I is an indicator function which is 1 if L_i is in S and 0 if L_i is not in S.

The LINK program has a very simple planning phase. The links are ordered according to the value of their likelihoods. This ordering would not affect Φ, the number of solutions, but it does insure that many of the poorer solutions are the last to be constructed, and under some circumstances, some partial solutions can be eliminated from consideration. Solutions are constructed by a structure generator as follows. One begins with a single solution S^0 with no links. The n ordered links are added one at a time to the solution space with i links, so that the solution space at $i + 1$, S^{i+1}, is equal to the j solutions of S^i, S_j^i, and up to j new solutions, S_j*^{i+1}. Each solution in S_j*^{i+1} equals one of the j solutions in S^i and the link L_{i+1}. The kth new solution, S_k*^{i+1}, exists if and only if the kth solution of S^i, S_k^i, is compatible with L_{i+1}.

The first heuristic used is derived from the fact that the links are ordered by score. By adding the highest scoring links first, one may arrive at a situation where the best solution after adding k links, S^k_{max}, has a score, $f(S^k_{max})$, greater than the score of some solution and the score of all the remaining links. That is,

$$f(S^k_{max}) > f(S^k_x) + \sum_{i=k+1}^{n} f(L_i) \qquad (10)$$

In this case S^k_x and all solutions with lower scores can be eliminated from the set of possible best solutions when forming the S^{k+1} solution space.

Two other heuristics are used in the LINK program. Using only the heuristic cited above guarantees that the best solution of the cluster will be found. The others do not guarantee that one will not end up in a local maximum, and are used only when necessary.

If a cluster is too large to be resolved by the above algorithm, then it must be broken down by accepting some very likely links or discarding some very unlikely links. This may resolve some sources of ambiguity and cause a large cluster to break into several smaller clusters.

The final heuristic is the pragmatic one, that the computer is limited in size, and that when the solution space in memory occupies a given size which is roughly a multiple of the number of solutions and the number of links per solution, some solutions must be eliminated. Rather than eliminating all of the lowest scoring partitions one might combine this strategy with trying to save the highest scoring of each family of solutions.

The cluster in Figure 5 may be used to illustrate the use of the link problem solver. Table 2 lists the links in the cluster, including the triangle link units. They are ordered by the arbitrary scores assigned to them, the comparison matrix of Table 3 is constructed, and the program begins to find solutions. After having added all six triangle links to the original null solution S^0, the solution space, S^6 has seven entries, the null solution and the six solutions each containing one triangle.

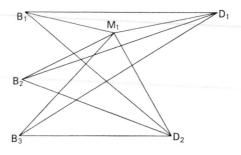

Figure 5

As the process advances from S^{10} to S^{11}, the null solution is eliminated as the null solution and the sum of the unused links is less than $f(S^{10}_{max})$. From this point on, the number of conceivable solutions has deletions at almost every stage of the process, and the final solution, L_1 and L_9 emerges. Again, in this example the best single link, L_7 is not part of the best overall solution.

Table 2 Ordered link scores for Figure 5

$B_2-M_1-D_1$	L_1	21
$B_3-M_1-D_2$	L_2	20
$B_3-M_1-D_1$	L_3	19
$B_1-M_1-D_2$	L_4	18
$B_2-M_1-D_2$	L_5	17
$B_1-M_1-D_1$	L_6	13
B_3-M_1	L_7	10
B_2-D_1	L_8	8
B_1-D_2	L_9	8
B_2-M_1	L_{10}	7
M_1-D_2	L_{11}	7
M_1-D_1	L_{12}	6
B_1-D_1	L_{13}	4
B_1-M_1	L_{14}	3
B_3-D_1	L_{15}	3
B_3-D_2	L_{16}	3
B_2-D_2	L_{17}	3

Table 3 Compatibility matrix for Figure 5

	1	2	3	4	5	6	7	8	9	10	11	12	13	14	15	16	17
1	0	1	1	1	1	1	1	1	0	1	1	1	1	1	1	1	0
2	1	0	1	1	1	1	1	0	1	1	1	1	0	1	1	1	1
3	1	1	0	1	1	1	1	1	0	1	1	1	1	1	1	0	1
4	1	1	1	0	1	1	1	0	1	1	1	1	1	1	0	1	1
5	1	1	1	1	0	1	1	1	1	1	1	1	0	1	0	1	1
6	1	1	1	1	1	0	1	1	1	1	1	1	1	1	1	0	0
7	1	1	1	1	1	1	0	0	0	1	1	1	0	1	1	0	1
8	1	0	1	0	1	1	0	0	0	1	0	1	1	0	1	1	0
9	0	1	0	1	1	1	0	0	0	0	1	0	1	1	0	1	1
10	1	1	1	1	1	1	1	1	0	0	1	1	0	1	0	1	0
11	1	1	1	1	1	1	1	0	1	1	0	1	0	1	0	1	1
12	1	1	1	1	1	1	1	1	0	1	1	0	1	1	1	0	0
13	1	0	1	1	0	1	0	1	1	0	0	1	0	1	1	0	0
14	1	1	1	1	1	1	1	0	1	1	1	1	0	0	0	0	0
15	1	1	1	0	0	1	1	1	0	0	0	1	1	0	0	0	1
16	1	1	0	1	1	0	0	1	1	1	1	0	0	0	0	0	1
17	0	1	1	1	1	0	1	0	1	0	1	0	0	0	1	1	0

THE FINAL PHASES OF RECORD LINKING

Once the clusters have been broken down, all of the links necessary for reconstitution will have been made. At this point, a revision program is run to establish the final genealogies to be accepted. During this last run the families formed are examined for logical consistency. For example, a family with one B, three BD, and one D child might actually be a four child family. The name may have changed in the records and the fourth BD link not made. Thus, records with name misspellings which were kept from linking are linked at this stage.

All of the above linking has been done on information digitally coded for the computer, with a unique code number representing each name, surname, parish, and related information. During the final phases, the computer would decode the information for those records which did not link satisfactorily but were grouped in the same sibship and see if the lack of linkage is due to the way in which information is coded. Since in Italy the names are spoken in dialect and recorded in either dialect, Italian, or Latin it is quite possible that changes in spelling keep records from linking. This phenomenon has been partially corrected for in the coding as diminutives have been coded in the same way as the full version of the name and some alternative spellings have been given the same coding. But when one adds the possibility of the priest misunderstanding the name as it is given to him, the existence of alternative spellings in different parishes, and the other forces which lead to considerable evolution in the names during the period of study, it becomes inevitable that some final stages of linking must be done on phonetically coded information.

The treatment of second marriages and illegitimate children has been left out of the discussion, but they do not present great difficulties. They may either be treated separately after the core of the genealogy is formed, or they may be considered with the other records by making a special M2 file for second marriages and a BI file for illegitimate births. In Italy such links are not difficult to make as the record itself indicates either second marriages or illegitimate birth.

CONCLUSION

With minor human intervention a computer can link parish records. Only in the final phases where linguistic interpretation occurs is manual intervention required. Eventually, if a computer could be programmed to interpret names phonetically and search for possible phonetic mutations of the information, mechanization could be completed. Although the method described in this chapter is designed specifically to link Italian parish records, it can be adapted to link within other similar data sets. As parish records exist for most Catholic and Protestant countries, the study of the historical population structure of much of the western world may be greatly extended using this source material.

Ian Winchester

6 A brief survey of the algorithmic, mathematical and philosophical literature relevant to historical record linkage

This survey consists of a discussion of the chief problems of record linkage which are relevant to historical data, followed by a select bibliography. The discussion takes the form of a critical survey of literature about record linkage.

INTRODUCTION

'Historical record linkage' is a phrase which means the bringing together of historical records referring to one and the same historical individual, regardless of whether the individual is a person, a family, a process, an event or an object. Historical record linkage is at least as old as written history, and, perhaps, as old as the human tradition of referring to individuals in the past in speech or action. Until recently the algorithmic, mathematical and philosophical problems associated with historical record linkage have lain submerged under a sea of historical practice. They have lain submerged simply because there was no good reason to raise them. The dual impacts of a quickening concern for social history, backed by convincing numerical argument and the increase in the employment of computer technology by historians (to handle census data, voters' lists, marriage record files, etc.) has raised this hidden three-fold hulk by supplying the reasons. In the following pages I will attempt to present the problems of record linkage as they arise in a historical context, and to summarize what is known about the problem in the published or distributed literature. Full bibliographical references will be found at the end of this chapter in the select bibliography of record linkage. Problems which have not yet been written about, but which seem to me to be important, will be presented but not discussed.

The problems of historical record linkage can be organized without too much overlap into three distinct categories: algorithmic problems, or problems concerned with practical record linkage procedures; mathematical problems, or problems concerned with the mathematical description of record linkage procedures and the statistical assumptions underlying them; and philosophical problems, mainly problems concerned with the descriptive metaphysics of historical individuation and reference. Under these three headings a number of distinct sub-problems arise. To these I will now turn.

ALGORITHMIC PROBLEMS OF HISTORICAL RECORD LINKAGE

Four problems stand out among the many involved in the linking of large files of records grouped into similar record types (for example, census rolls and assessment rolls). The first problem relates to the fact that the identifying items which one would like to employ to enable the identification of record pairs or multiple linkages are often changed, badly recorded or mis-reported. Among identifying items, proper names are specially important. Since they are also an item which, unlike other common identifying items (such as age, sex, religion, place of birth, etc.), are not usually descriptive items as well, these discrepancies lead to a special class of problems: the nominal record linkage problem.

The second general algorithmic problem is that of devising an overall strategy to enable the efficient linkage of records when large files of records are involved. Here, efficient algorithms are required for sorting records by some sorting key (such as alphabetically by surname) and for comparing individual record pairs, as well as for storing conveniently the linked pairs or multiple linkages which result. This is just as true whether the sorting, comparing or storing is done by hand, by a counter sorter or by a computer. Sorting (Iverson, 1962) is an expensive process, and one which must be taken seriously by every historian using large record files.

The third problem is how to organize a master file of linked records in such a manner that one can easily extract data which is historically interesting. This leads to a concern for such procedures as list-processing and to the question of compatibility between a file of linked records and various commercially available data analysis packages such as the Harvard Data-Text system and the Statistical Package for the Social Sciences (SPSS).

Finally, the fourth problem is that of deciding, in a given case, when one has a true link. Here the historian may find himself concerned on the one hand with such matters as the conditions under which full and less than full agreement in identifying items between linked records implies linkage. This can rapidly lead him into the difficult regions of weighting systems, degrees of hypothesis corroboration, and maximum likelihood test statistics. Or it may lead him into the still thornier thickets of devising an algorithm or algorithms to investigate networks of quasi-linked records in order to generate a 'best' linkage solution to the network according to some criterion chosen in advance. From this fourth general algorithmic problem stem the mathematical problems of record linkage. We will now discuss these general procedural problems in order.

I   IDENTIFYING ITEMS

(i) *Proper names*

Nearly every author in the field of record linkage has reported difficulties in handling names (Newcombe and Kennedy, 1962; Nitzberg and Sardy, 1965; Acheson, 1967; Winchester, 1970). Proper name linkage problems differ depending upon whether our concern is with the surname portion or the forename portion of the proper name. A number of authors have discovered that the surnames present in their data are often mis-reported, mis-spelled or changed or, perhaps, all three (Newcombe *et al.*, 1959; Nitzberg, 1968; Winchester, 1970). In some cases, for example with Scandinavian data linked according to family, surnames have variable postfixes (Peters*son*, Peters*dotter*) which depend upon the relationships between family members. In Iceland, even today (Magnus Magnusson, 1971) such surname transformations are present. In villages in Tuscany surnames were sometimes deliberately varied by family members in order to separate the various branches (see Herlihy's chapter in this volume). In some cases, surnames relating to one and the same person can be seen to have undergone definite changes describable as prefix, infix and postfix transformations which often follow a rational pattern (Winchester, 1970). Modern Swedish records suffer from the difficulty that people often change their names in order to avoid common names like Svenson, Petersson, Larsson. Consequently Sweden and the other Scandinavian countries employ a kind of substitute proper name, the birth number (Nielsen, 1968). Record linkage with records containing any of the above surname variations or changes requires special techniques.

The most commonly employed device to facilitate linkage of records when the surnames on two records may differ in spelling is that of the derived sorting key, such as the Soundex Code or the SINGS (Newcombe, 1967; Smith, 1968; Nitzberg, 1968; Winchester, 1970). The idea behind the derived sorting key technique is that if the least reliable letters in a surname are set aside and the others are coded, the abbreviated surname will be relatively error-free and almost as discriminating as the original name.

Another technique which may be necessary, particularly if the original data is in manuscript form (for example, manuscript censuses, parish registers) is a coding to overcome visual confusion. A written T or S can easily be confused in names like Leverton/ Severton. One Viewex code has been described and of course a combination of sound and visual coding is possible. In one case it was necessary to employ a triple combination of surname transformation pre-treatments, sound and visual coding (Winchester, 1970).

A very important concern connected with the devising and employing of a derived sorting key is that we wish to make as few record comparisons as possible, yet a coded surname sorting key naturally increases the number of records in a comparison set consisting of records with the same code. For example, Smith, Smythe, Smithe, Smithy, Smyth are all in the SMTH pocket if we simply drop vowels. This means more comparison candidates if we have a SMTH from another file we are trying to identify. One author (Newcombe, 1967), writing about a derived sorting key, has suggested analysing the factors involved in coding into two parts, the first representing the number of comparison sets the code permits, the other representing the efficiency of the code in eliminating discrepancies in cases of truly linked pairs. The ratio of these factors he terms a *merit ratio* for derived sorting keys. The higher the merit ratio the better the derived sorting key coding scheme since this means that more errors are eliminated with the least loss of discriminating power.

Another difficult problem connected with surnames is that in some cases there are a large number of individuals with the same surname in the file—even prior to coding. In English speaking countries the Smiths and Browns: in Sweden, the Svenssons. For such names as these, most of the identifying task falls to other identifying items. In the event that there are none or an inadequate number of these, either the would-be record linker must throw out a large part of his data or devise strategies for the 'best' allocation of linkage according to some prior statistical criterion. Only one author (Nathan, 1964) has done work in this difficult area. As the topic is intrinsically mathematical, this work will be discussed in the mathematical problem section following.

A final, and perhaps intractable, problem is that of name changes. For example, in one Swedish study involving immigrants to America in which two files of approximately 4,000 records each were to be linked, the problem of name changes was paramount.[1] It was common in Sweden to change names like Svensson to created names like Blomqvist (literally, flower twig) at the time of the major outmigration to America. Some 10 per cent of the records common to the two files involved such changes. The only solution at present available is to compare manually each unlinkable record in the first file with all the records in the second file to see if such a name change was the reason for difficulty in linkage. Since 40 per cent of the first file were unlinkable to the second, this meant that some 1,600 × 4,000 hand comparisons were made, i.e. 6·4 million.[2]

(ii) Other identifying items

Almost any kind of information item can function as an identifying item for record linkage purposes. The only condition is that it be present on more than one record relating to a particular historical individual. Naturally, other than proper names, such descriptive items as age, sex, place of birth, address, occupation and the like are the most frequently employed for identifying historical persons (Newcombe et al., 1959; Wrigley, 1966; Nitzberg, 1968; Tepping, 1968; Winchester, 1970). For other kinds of historical individuals other items would be required.

The fundamental treatment of the problems which may arise when using such items for identifying purposes is to be found in an article by Newcombe and Kennedy (1962). They report a number of identifying item discrepancies which they encountered in linking a file of British Columbia marriage records to a file of birth records during an investigation of possible human genetic changes due to radio-active fallout. Among the discrepancies encountered was the reversal in the initials for Christian names in pairs of records considered to be truly linked. As a solution to this problem, which had its analogue for other identifying items, Kennedy and Newcombe suggested a weighting scheme for identifying items which, provided certain prior probabilities could be estimated, gave a satisfactory and automatic solution to the problem of discrepancies in identifying items on truly linked pairs of records.

[1] Historiska Institutionen, Uppsala University, private communication, September 1971.
[2] This process is not complete at the time of writing, October 1971.

The discrepancies problem arises out of the fact that in the normal situation a pair of records is considered to relate to one and the same individual if and only if all the identifying items common to both records are identical. However since it is known that mis-reporting and mis-recording occur, a certain percentage of record pairs which are truly linked contain apparently discrepant identifying items. Equally, a certain percentage of record pairs which are linked according to the Identity of Indiscernibles principle must, in reality, relate to different individuals. The Kennedy and Newcombe procedure is to treat the linkage process as intrinsically probabilistic, assigning weights according to the degree to which the hypothesis that a record pair is linked is corroborated by the information in the records and a prior knowledge of records of the kinds involved. Weights are assigned according to the following formula:

1   weights are additive over identifying items
2   weights are calculated according to the formula

$$w_{i\text{-}th\ item} = \log_2 \frac{\text{Probability that item is in agreement (or disagreement) given linkage}}{\text{Probability a priori that item is in agreement (or disagreement) by chance}}$$

3   when weight total is above a certain 'cut-off' level, the record pair is considered as linked. Below the cut-off it is considered as unlinked.

This involves the assumption that the identifying items are statistically independent (for example, that age cannot be predicted, on the average, from a knowledge of, say, sex or address) and that a means exists for estimating, by appropriate frequency counts from some 'truly linked' file of specimen records the probability that a particular item is in agreement or disagreement on a truly linked record pair as opposed to the probability that the agreement or disagreement arises by chance.

Similar weighting systems are found employed in the more recent literature, all of which derive from the Kennedy and Newcombe work. One author employs the above system, but canvasses a number of other alternatives (Winchester, 1970). Felligi and Sunter (1967, 1969) have generalized the Kennedy and Newcombe weighting system treating the topic in the context of classical maximum likelihood statistical theory.

When the discrepancy in identifying items is not a severe problem other, simpler, systems may be employed. Thus Magnusson (1971) employs special test algorithms to check for initial reversals but does not use a weighting system. The binit weight strategy combined with special test algorithms is appropriate to many linkage situations which arise in a historical context, but requires extra effort to derive binit weights (since a hand linkage or some other equivalent error estimated procedure must be employed) and to program for the tests.

2   OVERALL LINKAGE STRATEGY

The problem of overall strategy can be considered conveniently by discussing certain characteristic problems. These depend upon such factors as the relative size of the files to be linked, the presence or absence of discrepancies in identifying items and the presence or absence of duplications of identifying item sets in the files to be linked. The cases of most importance in order of difficulty are:

1   No errors in identifying items and no duplication of identifying item sets.
2   No errors in identifying items and duplications of identifying item sets.
3   Errors in identifying items, but unique identifying item sets.
4   Errors in identifying items and duplications of identifying item sets.

Since nothing has been written on the difficulties engendered by various sizes of files, I will restrict myself to a discussion of these four cases, each of which is fairly well represented in the literature.

Case 1   The first case, in which there are assumed to be no errors in the identifying items and in which each identifying item set is represented uniquely in each file to be linked, is well represented in two recent studies. Drake (1971) in his study of mid-Victorian voting patterns and Bjarnason and others in their linkage of the national register, birth records, death records and blood group records in Iceland (Bjarnason *et al.*, 1968) apparently work with records which largely fulfill this requirement. With voters lists in nineteenth century Cambridge prior to the Secret Ballot Act of 1872 an elite sub-class of the population was canvassed and most of the individuals, their occupations and their political beliefs were well known and carefully recorded—often independently at the same time. Icelandic personal data has been carefully kept by the families themselves and most families retain a family genealogy book which is passed on from generation to generation. According to Magnusson it is possible at present, in any linkage situation in which a doubt arises about any individual born in this century, to call up the family concerned on the telephone (Magnusson, 1971). This eliminates problems of errors in identifying information and lack of uniqueness in identifying items.

Cases such as these permit a straightforward linkage scheme to be employed involving two basic steps:

1   sorting the records by surname and other identifying items
2   merging the records from the files to be linked.

Because the identifying item sets are unique and there are no errors in identifying items, these two operations ought to bring together all the records which refer to the same individual. In the ideal case, it is logically irrelevant which operation is performed first, although there are good practical reasons for sorting each file first and then merging the files. Most computer systems possess built in facilities for the operations of sorting and merging. Consequently, if a historian considers his data sufficiently clean in the sense of containing extremely well recorded descriptive items and unique identifying item sets, automated record linkage can be performed quickly for pairs of record files. As we shall see, sorting and merging, although the basic steps involved in linking file pairs with large numbers of records, are not sufficient to cope with linkages involving several files. But for a great many record linkage operations used in nineteenth century studies, sorting and merging are the basic steps. For each of the other three cases in this section linkage strategy consists of refining and extending the basic sort/merge schema in order to handle specific difficulties.

Case 2   The second case, in which we assume no errors in identifying items but duplication of identifying item sets is often encountered in practice in magazine subscription billing problems. In cities which like New York have many large apartment buildings, it may happen that there is more than one person in such a building with the name William Brown with a subscription to, say, the Reader's Digest. If the address recorded gives only the number of the building, then special procedures are required for allocating bills so that on the average the company collects the most money at the least billing cost (a statistical approach to subscription lists is feasible when several million copies are sold). This problem has been studied in considerable detail by Nathan (1964, 1967) and Tepping (1955, 1958). An application of

Nathan's scheme may be found in the Swedish study of people's political movements in the late nineteenth and early twentieth century (Andrae and Lundqvist, 1969). Swedish data has the peculiar property that a very high percentage of the population have the post-fix 'son' (Petersson, Andersson, Svensson, Carlsson, Johansson etc.). This means that it is likely that duplicate identifying item sets refer-ring to different persons may be found in each file to be linked. In such a case, the alternatives are to throw away the data which contains duplicates or accept a statistical solution which is in some sense best. For studies of popular political movements, casting out the common surnames is to be avoided if possible. In practice, this would mean following a scheme like that which Nathan has devised. The funda-mental modification to the overall scheme of (a) sorting and (b) merging is to add a third basic step, namely, allocating linkages according to a statistically best scheme in cases of duplication of identifying item sets. In practice this means making some linkages randomly. Nathan's contribution is to have devised a means of estimating the outcome probabilities for various pathways in a linkage algorithm which contains as one of its branches a random allocator.

Case 3   The third case, in which we assume errors in identifying item sets, but assume uniqueness of these sets, occurs in studies using nineteenth century record files. Thus the files described in the Hamilton Project (Katz, 1970) are representative of this kind of linkage problem, as are most of those employed by the various authors in *Nineteenth century cities*.[3] Many of the problems of this case were discussed above in connection with name variations and derived sorting keys, though solutions to these problems may need to be extended to cover other identifying items in linked pairs.

One solution has been devised by Kennedy and Newcombe. The problem which Newcombe posed to Kennedy was that of finding a rapid and convenient means for linking the marriage, birth and death records of the Canadian province of British Columbia. A very extensive preliminary hand study of the records indicated that they were exceptionally clean and potentially useful for genetic purposes since the death records contained cause of death and since handi-capped persons were routinely recorded. As the records were in such a good state, linkage was accomplished in a large percentage of cases merely by sorting the records by a double Soundex code employing the surnames of both parents on the birth and death records and of the married couple in the case of marriage records. In many linkage

[3] Thernstrom, S. (ed.), *Nineteenth century cities* (Newhaven and London, 1970).

situations there was only one candidate for linkage in a double Soundex comparison set. In most of the cases in which there were more than a single candidate for linkage in such a comparison set, one candidate only had all identifying items in agreement with the incoming record. For the few cases left over, the binit weighting system sufficed to identify the true linkage partner.

Airline passenger identification systems also assume the case of no duplication of identifying item sets but errors in identifying items (Davidson, 1962). The problem here differs from the previous situation in that the data handling is in real time, i.e. is a moment to moment record linkage operation. This cannot be performed except by third generation multiple access computers or special systems designed solely for data retrieval. As linkage in the case of airline passengers is mainly achieved by surname matching, algorithms have been devised for the weighting of degrees of likeness of surnames according to one of many possible schemes. For example, Davidson's scheme employs two steps: name compression and comparison-and-weighting. The name compression step consists simply of deleting the vowels. The comparison and weighting step consists in assigning a weight according to the degree to which the class of letters in one surname is included in the class of letters in the other.

Case 4   The most difficult case, and the one which is almost always present in small numbers in any linkage operation is the case of errors in identifying items and multiplicity of identifying item sets. This case has not received special treatment in the literature, although all large record linkage operations must take account of this case in some manner or other. In principle, the difficulty could be met by combining methods described in cases 2 and 3: first a weight is assigned to each potential linkage and then some allocation algorithm employed in the case of duplications. The problem is complicated by the fact that it may present itself in two ways. The first is where there are a number of equally good candidates for linkage in the sense of their all being assigned the same linkage weight. Second is where there are equally good candidates for linkage in the sense of their possessing an identical identifying item set. Little has so far been written on these issues. In the case of the system Winch73 devised for the Hamilton Project, these two cases were conflated and the numerically first record pair was chosen in all instances (Katz, 1970). A more prudent course would have been to suspend a linkage decision in all such cases and search for more information.

A highly important consideration which this case forces to light is the *cost* of various actions under conditions of uncertainty in linkage systems. A contribution to this question has been made by Tepping, who considers a model for estimating the costs of various linkage 'actions' such as (a) treating a pair of records as linked (b) temporarily treating a pair of records as linked but obtaining additional information before finally classifying, (c) taking no action immediately and obtaining additional information, (d) temporarily treating a pair as a non link and obtaining more information, (e) treating a pair as a non link (Tepping, 1968). Essentially Tepping's model assumes an iterative linkage procedure is available to the researcher, and that the unit cost of each action can be estimated.

3   FILE ORGANIZATION

So far the literature of record linkage only describes two main ways of organizing record files, the card index method and the list processing method. As there are many different file organization problems and as file size is often the major problem in organizing a record linkage operation, this is perhaps surprising. Again, it is Kennedy who has done the most thinking in this field and his Chalk River and Oxford articles are clearly and boldly written (Kennedy, 1964, 1968). Both those historians who are concerned to reconstitute families from parish records and those who are using census and assessment rolls and the like can benefit from his experience and masterly exposition.

As it is only large file linkage operations that require automated or semi-automated methods, and as costs are largely governed by the amount of computer core (central processor) time used, a file must be organized in a manner that minimizes copying and recopying whole subfiles of records in core. In record linkage operations carried out by hand, it is often convenient merely to order a file in some manner with the individual records in the form of a deck of Hollerith punch cards. When a linkage is found, the new record is added to the old file by inserting the new record between two old ones. Although this operation can be simulated in a digital computer it is a clumsy operation for a computer to perform. This is because, while it is easy for a human merely to separate a pair of physical records with a thumb and slip a new record between them, for a computer to do the equivalent operation each record below the point of insertion must be shifted backwards one place. This requires that all of the records below the insertion be copied via the central processor to a working space, the new record inserted and then the records in the working space replaced one record back on the original file. Clearly, an operation which is easy for a historian to perform just sitting at his desk is very costly for a computer to perform.

Kennedy's suggestion for the organization of computer linked record files is that we ignore the process which is easiest for a man to perform and look at what the computer can do most conveniently. A computer can easily be programmed to keep track of a file organization cross-referencing scheme. Kennedy suggested, therefore, that a master file of linked records be formed by presorting all the records in the files to be linked into what he termed 'superfamilies' of records consisting of all the Smiths or Browns or Svenssons in the combined files. Each record in the superfamily was given a unique number according to its physical position in the master file. From this point onward, the physical location of the records in the master file was fixed. However, the relationships between records in the master file could be changed by means of crossreferencing information associated with the records in the file. Essentially Kennedy suggested replacing changes in the physical order of the file by changes in the logical order of the file. A very readable exposition of this technique is given by Newcombe (1967).

In his most recent work Kennedy investigated the technical difficulties involved in building up large and complex files of multi-generational family structures (Kennedy, 1968). His discussion is of exceptional interest to historians working with family reconstitution methods. Kennedy concluded that, in principle, there is no theoretical barrier to building up such files for whole populations, but that no third generation computers have adequate storage capacities for the task except for small files. He also gives many useful suggestions for extracting pedigree data from a linked file.

The problem of complex file organization is becoming increasingly important and topical due to the ever expanding employment of family reconstitution methods in social history. In particular, Wrigley has given considerable thought to this problem in the process of automating the reconstitution methods employed by the *Cambridge Group for the History of Population and Social Structure* (Wrigley, 1966, and the chapter by Wrigley and Schofield in this volume). From work of this type we may expect to see the next major contributions to this topic.

4 CHOICE OF WEIGHTING SYSTEMS AND ESTIMATION OF WEIGHTS

A historian who is contemplating automating his record linkage operation and who finds that his case is that of Case 3 or Case 4 of the section on overall linkage strategy will find himself puzzling over whether or not to use a weighting system like that of Kennedy, and if so, which weighting system he ought to employ. Generally speaking, whether or not a weighting system should be employed will depend upon two factors: (a) how clean the files are and (b) how much money and effort the historian can make available. A wise maxim to follow is to use the simplest possible method which can accomplish the job in hand. The simpler the method the more quickly useful results can be obtained.

How can one discover how 'clean' a file is? Only by linking a sample of the files in question by hand (perhaps with the help of a card sorter). If, say, 25 to 50 per cent of the linkages involve discrepant identifying items the files are 'dirty'. The historian must then ask himself whether or not he can afford to throw away 25 to 50 per cent of his linked file and still establish anything important. If the files are rather clean in the sense that very few discrepancies in identifying items occur on hand linked pairs he may, as with the Scottish Psychiatric Case Register Study (Robertson, *et al.*, 1969) or the Iceland study (Bjarnason *et al.*, 1968) employ a simple linkage technique using a card sorter or a sorting and merging operation using a computer.

If the files are not 'clean', but it seems unacceptable to throw away linked pairs, then an expensive and complex linkage system which includes a weighting technique will be necessary. But which weighting system? And how should the actual weights be employed? There are three published discussions of weighting systems (Kennedy *et al.*, 1964; Felligi and Sunter, 1969; Winchester, 1970). Kennedy relates his weighting system to the concept of information and asks: how much information do we gain through the comparison of identifying items on a potentially linked record pair as opposed to our *a priori* knowledge of the probability that the pair may be linked by chance? He constructs a ratio of probabilities:

$$\frac{P(\text{linkage given particular agreements and disagreements in identifying items})}{P(\text{linkage of the record pair by chance})} = \frac{P(L/G)}{P(L)}$$

the logarithm (to the base 2) of this expression is the weight. Felligi and Sunter ask: by how much does the probability of a particular set of agreements and disagreements in an identifying item set when a pair is linked differ from the probability of the same set of agreements and disagreements arising when the pair of records is not linked?

They consequently construct a ratio of likelihoods of the form:

$$\frac{P\left(\begin{array}{l}\text{particular agreements and disagree-}\\ \text{ments in identifying items}\end{array}\Big|\begin{array}{l}\text{given}\\\text{linkage}\end{array}\right)}{P\left(\begin{array}{l}\text{particular agreements and disagree-}\\ \text{ments in identifying items}\end{array}\Big|\begin{array}{l}\text{given}\\\text{non-linkage}\end{array}\right)} = \frac{P(G/L)}{P(G/-L)}$$

to serve as a weight. They also consider it convenient to employ the logarithm of this measure. Winchester points out that a number of weighting systems are available drawn from common sense and from the literature of hypothesis corroboration as well as from classical statistical theory, and indicates that under some conditions a simple scoring system may be adequate (for example, scoring $+1$ for an agreement in identifying items and -1 for disagreements). His general approach is that of hypothesis corroboration. Thus his basic question is: to what degree does the evidence internal to the records plus our background knowledge of the types of linkage situation under consideration lead to a corroboration of the hypothesis that the record pair in question are linked? There is little to choose between the three approaches, and with a little word play they can be reduced to one another. In these circumstances simplicity is often best.

To derive weights, therefore, one must estimate a number of partial probabilities and *a priori* probabilities. The *a priori* probabilities can be based on frequency counts from the raw files. Partial probabilities may be derived from raw files under certain circumstances (Felligi and Sunter, 1969; and Du Bois, 1969), but may well entail generating a small hand linked sample.

MATHEMATICAL PROBLEMS OF HISTORICAL RECORD LINKAGE

Discussing weighting systems has already involved touching on some mathematical problems of historical record linkage. The mathematical description of record linkage processes may mean using terms and expressions unfamiliar to the non-mathematician. In the next few pages I will try to convey the general mathematical problems and results in the field without launching into symbols.[4]

---

[4] Doubtless there will be historians who will consider this restraint regrettable, just as there will be those who will consider the following comments much too technical.

The mathematical problems of record linkage can conveniently be divided into two general problems:

1 the description of linkage processes involving the linkage of two record files, and
2 the description of linkage involving complex networks of potentially linkable records which require resolution.

These two general problems correspond roughly to the two great present day record linkage interests among historians, namely (a) the linkage of files of nineteenth century census records, assessment rolls, voters' lists, etc. and (b) family reconstitution from parish registers.

1 THEORIES OF TWO-FILE RECORD LINKAGE

Theories of two-file record linkage are designed to lead to optimal linkage rules under special assumptions concerning the files in question. In practice, although real files never quite meet these mathematical assumptions, they may come close to doing so.

There are three basic approaches to the problem of describing mathematically a two-file linkage process. Felligi and Sunter assume that the probabilities of erroneous matches and non-matches are fixed in advance and seek to minimize the number of cases for which no decision is made (Felligi and Sunter, 1967, 1969). Their reason for this approach is that such cases are costly since they may involve a complicated hand matching process and later updating of the files. Du Bois, on the other hand, attempts to maximize the set of correct matches while minimizing erroneous matches (Du Bois, 1965, 1969). The third approach is to attempt to minimize a cost function which can be specified in advance (Nathan, 1967; Tepping, 1968).

Without reproducing the actual mathematical work of these authors it is difficult to convey *how* they arrive at their results. However it is possible to describe their descriptive assumptions and their optimization criteria.

Felligi and Sunter begin by assuming two populations of individuals which they call A and B. The individual members of these are called a_i and b_i respectively. They assume that at least some individuals are common to A and B so that, if we lump both populations together, we can consider the lumped population as consisting of a matched set of individuals and an unmatched set. The matched set of individuals are referred to as M and the unmatched set are referred to as U (see Figure 1).

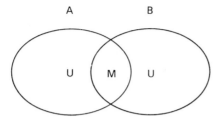

Figure 1

A added to $B = M$ added to U, and nobody is left over. Next, it is assumed that each individual member of the population has some descriptive characteristics associated with it. Finally, it is assumed that there are two record generating processes, one for each population, which produces a single record for each member of each population containing some selected characteristics. The record generating process also introduces some errors and some incompleteness in the resulting records. As a result, two unmatched members of A and B may give rise to identical records and, conversely, two matched (identical) members of A and B may give rise to different records.

The first step in trying to link the records of the two files (i.e. identifying the records which correspond to matched members of A and B) is to compare the records. This results in a set of codes for such statements as 'name is the same', 'name is the same and it is Abernathy', 'name missing on one record', 'age disagrees', etc. This set of codes, written out as a string, is called by Felligi and Sunter the *comparison vector* for a particular linkage attempt (Felligi and Sunter, 1969). In the course of the linkage operation we observe the comparison vector and want to decide on the basis of the evidence contained in it whether or not a_i and b_i are a matched pair or an unmatched pair. The decision that they are a matched pair is symbolized as A_1 (action one) by our authors, and is also termed a *positive link*. The decision that they are an unmatched pair is symbolized by A_3 and is termed a *positive non-link*. The next fundamental assumption which is made is that 'There will be some cases in which we shall find ourselves unable to make either of these decisions *at specified levels of error* (my italics) . . . so that we allow a third decision, denoted A_2, a *possible link*.'

The object of developing this descriptive theory is to find an unambiguous means of maximizing the assignments of positive links and positive non-links at specified levels of error, by means of some appropriately chosen linkage rule. What do Felligi and Sunter mean by the terms linkage rule and levels of error associated with their linkage rule? It will be recalled that the record generating process was assumed to produce records which, on occasion, gave rise to identical records relating to two unmatched members of A and B and vice-versa. The frequency with which the record generating process in combination with the linkage rule produced these two types of errors are the levels of errors which Felligi and Sunter mean. The first kind of error is called mu and the second lambda in their terminology. A linkage rule is a rule which specifies in each case of the comparison vector whether to take action A_1, A_2 or A_3. It is not hard to see that by varying the linkage rule we can increase or decrease the number of errors which we let slip through, so that the probability that we accept as linked a pair of records which are, in reality, unmatched and the probability that we treat as non-linked a pair of records which, in reality, refer to one and the same individual depends on the rules we employ to decide which of the three actions to take. What is an *optimal linkage rule*?

According to Felligi and Sunter it is one which maximizes the positive dispositions (i.e. decisions A_1 and A_3) subject to fixed levels of error mu and lambda, chosen in advance. The idea is to minimize the number of cases in which we cannot make a positive disposition and must abandon the linkage attempt as it stands and search for more information about the individuals being linked.

Felligi and Sunter succeeded in formulating a linkage rule which meets these requirements. Figure 2 illustrates their solution. In it the

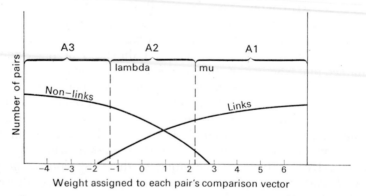

Figure 2

vertical axis measures the number of linked pairs or of non-linked pairs, while the horizontal axis measures the weights attached to the comparison vectors of record pairs. The line sloping down from the left indicates the number of positively non-linked pairs assigned particular weights according to their comparison vectors. The line sloping down from the right indicates the number of positively linked pairs similarly. The line marked mu corresponds to the preset level of error for linked pairs which are treated by a linkage rule as non-linked. The line marked lambda corresponds to the present level of error for non-linked pairs which are treated as linked. The linkage rule which is optimal in this case is to accept as a positive link any comparison vector with a weight greater than that corresponding to mu and to treat as a positive non-link any comparison vector with a weight less than lambda. If mu and lambda were placed together on the diagram, then only actions A_1 and A_3 would be possible. As the diagram is presently arranged, all of the cases which lie between mu and lambda are undecided (i.e. are A_2 cases).

By using the same descriptive assumptions, but disagreeing as regards the object of linkage, it is possible to devise other linkage rules which are optimum on the basis of other criteria. For example, one might attempt to determine the point at which the two curves in the diagram above cross. This would correspond to considering as optimum the maximization of positive linkage dispositions with the simultaneous minimization of positive non-linkage dispositions. This is the essence of the theory of Du Bois.

Another possibility would be to attempt to maximize the number of positive linkages alone. For example, a government might consider that it is important to identify all criminals, even if some innocent people are also identified as criminals. This would correspond to the linkage rule of trying to find the point at which the linkages curve crossed the horizontal axis. In the diagram above this is roughly at -2. On the other hand, if a government considered it important to make sure that no innocent persons were ever identified as criminals then an optimum linkage rule would be when the non-links curve crossed the horizontal axis, roughly at $+3$ in our diagram. Or again, if the cost of the various dispositions A_1, A_2 and A_3 markedly differed and we wished to minimize the total cost of the operation, regardless of error levels, then another linkage rule would have to be devised. Those who are interested in these sorts of optimizations should turn to the work of Tepping and Nathan.

2   MULTIPLE FILE LINKAGE

The theories outlined above consider only linkage systems involving two files. The work of Kennedy and Newcombe, as well as that of the authors just discussed, implicitly assumes that the problem for N-files of records may be solved simply by decomposing the N-file problem into N-1 separate two-file linkage operations. That this assumption is not, in general, valid can be seen by considering the problems of linkage with records drawn from three files.

We then have three records a, b, c for comparison which may or may not relate to one and the same individual. With respect to identifying item sets on the three records, three cases are possible.

1   All three records have the same identifying items
2   The three records have overlapping identifying item sets
3   Each record has identifying item sets which overlap with only one other record.

The essence of record linkage from a historical point of view is that the possibility of linking records relating to historical individuals should in appropriate cases lead to the conclusion that the records relate to one and the same individual, i.e. that the individuals to which the records relate are identical. Ideally, we would like to treat the linkage relation as transitive, so that if record a is linked to record b, and record b is linked to record c, we are entitled to infer that record a is linked to record c. The possibility of errors in the identifying item sets means that we cannot simply assume this ideal situation. We must specify linkage rules which say when we are entitled to infer from atomic linkages of the form a–L–B and b–L–c to the molecular linkage a—L—b. The linkage rules specified by

$$a \overset{\displaystyle L \qquad L}{\underset{\displaystyle c}{\diagdown \diagup}} b$$

Felligi and Sunter or by Du Bois and others give us no guidance in such cases. For example, using the terminology of Figure 2 it is possible that the linkage a—L—b is assigned a high weight beyond a pairwise cut-off level mu_1 and that b–L–c is also assigned a high weight beyond the pairwise cut-off level mu_2, but that a–L–c is assigned a weight below the pairwise cut-off level $lambda_3$. What are we to do in such a case? Which linkages are we to include? Current discussions do not even recognize that such cases exist.

We can diagram the three cases of overlap in identifying item sets as follows:

Identifying items

	a	b	c	d	e	f	g	h	i	j	k	l	m	n	o	p	q	
Case 1	–	–	–	–	–	–												Record a
	–	–	–	–	–	–												„ b
	–	–	–	–	–	–												„ c
Case 2	–	–	–	–	–	–	–	–										Record a
			–	–	–	–	–	–	–	–								„ b
					–	–	–	–	–	–	–	–						„ c
Case 3	–	–	–	–	–	–	–	–										Record a
			–	–	–	–	–	–	–	–	–	–						„ b
							–	–	–	–	–	–						„ c

Figure 3

In Case 1, each of *a*, *b* and *c* have the same identifying items. In Case 2, while there is overlap in identifying items between all three records, between *a* and *c* there is very little overlap and possibly not enough to establish a direct linkage between *a* and *c*. In Case 3, no identifying items overlap between *a* and *c*, which means that if we wish to consider *a*, *b* and *c* as referring to one and the same historical individual, it must be via an inference of the form *a–L–b* and *b–L–c* entails *a——L——b*. If we are employing a weighting system in

order to generate linked triples of records, clearly even if all of the possible identifying items agree in Cases 2 and 3 the weight assigned directly to *a–L–c* is in Case 2 bound to be a low weight and in Case 3, no weight at all can be assigned.

A general question then arises for cases of multiple linkages, namely, *under what circumstances we are entitled to infer from atomic linkages* (i.e. pairwise linkages) *in combination the corresponding molecular linkage.*

Consideration of this general question forces us to consider certain interrelated diagrams such as those shown in Figure 4 for four-record networks. In this figure points represent records and lines represent links between records.[5] In terms of the general question above, a linkage rule for the four-record case should specify under what circumstances we are entitled to infer the complete quadruple linkage

[5] As Wrigley points out, since demographic records are ordered in time, a more accurate description of the linkage relation between records is that of a digraph. The logical relation to which all such record linkages point is the relation between individuals, 'is the same *X* as', (e.g. 'belongs to the same family as', 'is the very same person as', 'belongs to the same event as', etc.), which is symmetric and transitive.

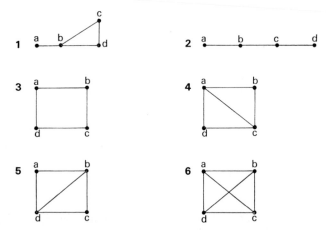

Figure 4

(6) from the various possible combinations of linked pairs and triples, as in (1) to (5).

Wrigley and Schofield and Skolnick have considered this question (as appears in chapters 4 and 5 of this volume). The diagrams in Figure 4 are called graphs in the jargon of the mathematician (in this connection see especially Harary *et al.*, 1965, and Harary, 1969).

Unfortunately for multiple file linkage questions, the general theorems of graph theory are relatively few, due to the fact that a great deal of the theory stems from an attempt to handle one of the great unsolved problems of mathematics, the classical map problem.

In practice, the problem of inference to completely linked groups of records is considerably more complex than the diagrams of Figure 4 suggest. This is due to the fact that there may often be multiple candidates for linkage and hence more than one network of the forms (1) to (5) available requiring possible inference to the complete quadruple (6).

Family reconstitution problems and genetic problems (Wrigley, 1966; Barrai, Moroni and Cavalli-Sforza, 1968) may often lead to very complex networks of potentially linked records which must be resolved. In order to resolve such networks a reasonable first step is to identify all of the subordinate potentially completely linked *n*-tuples such as (6) above in the network. Other than a method of exhaustion, there are no rapid ways of identifying such complete sub-graphs of the network. This means that for very large networks the computer time needed merely to identify potentially linked *n*-tuples is prohibitive. The same difficulty arises in other situations which can be described by the theory of graphs, for example the examination scheduling problem.

Identifying all of the conflicts between groups of n courses in the context of examination scheduling is a problem analogous to the network resolution problem. The difficulties of scheduling examinations in the minimum number of periods is analogous in difficulty to that of optimally resolving complex networks of potentially linked records. Unfortunately, other than exhaustion, no algorithms exist for the examination scheduling problem which work under any but severely restricted circumstances.

PHILOSOPHICAL PROBLEMS OF HISTORICAL RECORD LINKAGE

There is a sense in which one may consider the debate over the optimum linkage rules a philosophical debate. Many of the issues within the debate are technical and will ultimately be decided by mathematical considerations. There are, however a number of problems which record linkage theory and practice bring to light which will never be decided by mathematical theory. I have in mind such questions as the following:

1 What is involved in making a historical reference and what are the general conditions under which a historical reference may be successfully brought about?

2 Under what circumstances are we entitled to say that we have successfully identified a historical individual? Under what circumstances are we justified in concluding that a particular historical individual existed?

3 What general process or processes underlies the growth of historical knowledge—if any?

Note that the model of record linkage presented by Felligi and Sunter assumed in advance that there were two populations of historical individuals, A and B and that there were records corresponding to each individual a_1 of A and to each individual b_1 of B. They also assumed that in the process of record generation some errors, misrecordings, misreportings and the like occurred. Consequently, according to their model, it may happen in a particular instance that a pair of records which in reality refer to one and the same historical individual nonetheless contain discrepant identifying items. And conversely, it may happen that a pair of records which are indistinguishable as regards identifying items in reality refer to different individuals. The philosophical problem is this. How are we ever to be sure, in a particular case, that the pair of records we are treating as truly linked are not, in reality, just a case of compensating errors and vice versa? This line of reasoning, if pressed to its logical conclusion, would lead to an intolerable scepticism concerning the possibility of true reference in history at all. Consequently we are led to ask fundamental questions concerning the descriptive metaphysics of historical reference in record linkage contexts.

This problem may seem remote from everyday historical work, but since all historical contexts involve implicit record linkage operations, the problem cannot be shrugged away.

Finally, a word about the growth of historical knowledge. In the section of this appendix in which three cases for the overlap of identifying item sets between three records to be linked was presented, it became clear that in order for something *new* to be said, records must be linked which contain descriptive items above and beyond the items employed for identifying purposes. That is, for the growth of historical knowledge record linkage operations and inferences to n-tuple linkage situations are implicitly involved in which the identifying item sets on the records involved do not necessarily overlap. This leads to a record linkage account of the processes underlying the growth of historical knowledge. It also leads to just those sceptical difficulties involved in making inferences via the assumed transitivity of the linkage relation.

On the theory of reference in general, the interested reader might begin with the work of Russell, Frege and Strawson. (Russell, 1905; Strawson, 1950; Frege, 1970). On the topic of the growth of scientific knowledge in general he may consult Popper and Kuhn (Popper, 1968; Kuhn, 1962). I have attempted to clarify some of the more particular problems in a recent article (Winchester, 1970).

A select bibliography of record linkage

Note: an asterisk beside an entry indicates that the entry
is very useful

ACHESON, E. D., 'The Oxford Record Linkage Study. A review of
the method with some preliminary results', *Proceedings of the Royal
Society of Medicine*, 57 (1964), 11

*ACHESON, E. D., *Medical record linkage* (Oxford, 1967)

ACHESON, E. D. (ed.), *Record linkage in medicine* (Edinburgh and
London, 1968)

ANDRAE, C. G. and LUNDQVIST, S., 'Folkrörelserna och den svenska
demokratiserings processen', *Historisk Tidskrift* (1969), 197–
214

BJARNASON, O., FRIDRIKSSON, S., and MAGNUSSON, M., 'Record
linkage in a self-contained community', in Acheson, E. D. (ed.),
Record linkage in medicine (Edinburgh and London, 1968), 62–69

BARRAI, I., MORONI, A., and CAVALLI-SFORZA, L. L., 'Further
studies in record linkage from parish books', in Acheson, E. D.
(ed.), *Record linkage in medicine* (Edinburgh and London, 1968),
270–82

DAVIDSON, L., 'Retrieval of misspelled names in an airline passenger record system', *Communications of the Association for Computing Machinery*, 5 (1962), 169–71

DRAKE, M., 'The mid-Victorian voter', *Journal of Interdisciplinary
History*, 1 (1971), 473–90

DU BOIS, N. S. D., 'A document linkage program for digital computer', *Behavioural Science*, 10 (1965), 312–19

DU BOIS, N. S. D., 'A solution to the problem of linking multivariate
documents', *Journal of American Statistical Association*, 64 (1969),
163–74

FELLIGI, I. P., and SUNTER, A. B., 'An optimal theory of record linkage', *Proceedings of the International Symposium on Automation of Population Register Systems*, vol. I (Jerusalem, 1967)

*FELLIGI, I. P., and SUNTER, A. B., 'A theory for record linkage', *Journal of the American Statistical Association*, 64 (1969), 1183–1210

FLEURY, M., and HENRY, L., *Des registres paroissiaux à l'histoire de la population. Manuel de dépouillement et d'exploitation de l'état civil ancien* (Paris, 1956)

FREGE, G., 'On sense and reference', in *Philosophical writings of Gottlob Frege*, Geach and Black (trans.) (Oxford, 1970), 56–78

GOODMAN, L. A., 'On the estimation of the number of classes in a population', *Annals of Mathematical Statistics*, 20 (1949), 572–9

GOODMAN, L. A., 'On the analysis of samples from k lists', *Annals of Mathematical Statistics*, 23 (1952), 632–4

GURALNICK, L., and NAM, C. B., 'Census-N.O.U.S. study of death certificates matched to census records', *Milbank Memorial Fund Quarterly*, 37 (1959), 144–53

HARARY, F., *Graph theory* (Reading, Mass. and elsewhere, 1969)

HARARY, F., NORMAN, R. Z., and CARTWRIGHT, D., *Structural models: an introduction to the theory of directed graphs* (New York, 1965)

HAUSER, P. M., and LAURIAT, P., 'Record matching—theory and practice', *Proceedings of the Social Statistics Section, American Statistical Association* (1963), 25

*IVERSON, K. E., *A programming language* (New York, 1962)

KATZ, M. B., 'Social structure in Hamilton, Ontario', in Thernstrom, S. (ed.), *Nineteenth century cities* (New Haven and London, 1969), 209–44

KATZ, M. B. (ed.), *The Hamilton Project: an interim report*, no. 2 Department of History and Philosophy of Education, Ontario Institute for Studies in Education, Nov. 1970

*KENNEDY, J. M. *Linkage of birth and marriage records using a digital computer*, Document No. AECL-1258, Atomic Energy of Canada Limited, Chalk River, Ontario (1961)

KENNEDY, J. M., 'The use of a digital computer for record linkage', *The use of vital and health statistics for genetic and radiation studies*, U.N. publication, Sales no. 61, XVII, i (1962), 155–60

*KENNEDY, J. M., 'File structures for the automatic manipulation of linked records', in Acheson, E. D. (ed.), *Record linkage in medicine* (Edinburgh and London, 1968), 109–19

*KENNEDY, J. M., et al., 'List processing methods for organizing files of linked records', Document No. AECL-2078, Atomic Energy of Canada Limited, Chalk River, Ontario (1964)

KUHN, T. S., *The structure of scientific revolutions* (Chicago, 1962)

LAKATOS, I. and MUSGRAVE, A. (eds.), *Criticism and the growth of knowledge* (Cambridge, 1970)

MAGNUSSON, M., 'Computer methods for the linkage of the national register, birth records, death records and blood group records in Iceland', paper distributed at the Nominal Record Linkage Conference, Princeton, May, 1971

NATHAN, GAD, 'On optimal matching processes', Ph.D. dissertation, Case Institute of Technology, Cleveland, Ohio, 1964

NATHAN, GAD, 'Outcome probabilities for a record matching process with complete invariant information', *Journal of American Statistical Association*, 62 (1967), 454–69

NEWCOMBE, H. B., 'Record linking. The design of efficient systems for linking records into individual and family histories', *American Journal for Human Genetics*, 19 (1967), 335–59

NEWCOMBE, H. B. (I) 'Products from the early stages in the development of a system of linked records', and (II) 'Multi-generation pedigrees from linked records', in Acheson, E. D. (ed.), *Record linkage in medicine* (Edinburgh and London, 1968), 7–34 and 295–303

*NEWCOMBE, H. B., and KENNEDY, J. M., 'Record linkage: making maximum use of the discriminating power of identifying information', *Communications of the Association for Computing Machinery*, 5 (1962), 563–5

NEWCOMBE, H. B., KENNEDY, J. M., AXFORD, S. L., and JAMES, A. P., 'Automatic linkage of vital records', *Science*, 130 (1959), 954–9

NEWCOMBE, H. B., and RHYNAS, P. O. W., 'Family linkage of population records', *The use of vital and health statistics for genetic and radiation studies*, U.N. publication, Sales no. 61, XVII, i (1962), 135–54

NEWCOMBE, H. B., and RHYNAS, P. O. W., 'Child spacing following stillborn and infant death', *Eugenics Quarterly*, 9 (1962), 23–35

NIELSEN, H., 'The personal numbering system in Denmark', in Acheson, E. D. (ed.), *Record linkage in medicine* (Edinburgh and London, 1968), 173–9

NITZBERG, D. M., 'Results of research into the methodology of record linkage', in Acheson, E. D. (ed.), *Record linkage in medicine* (Edinburgh and London, 1968), 187–204

NITZBERG, D. M., and SARDY, H., 'The methodology of computer linkage of health and vital records', *Proceedings of the Social Statistics Section, American Statistical Association*, (1965), 100

POPPER, K. R., *The logic of scientific discovery* (London, 1968)

RAEL, P. G., and PETERSON, R. P., 'A solution to the problem of optimum classification', *Annals of Mathematical Statistics*, 20 (1949), 433–8

RAO, C. R., 'A general theory of discrimination when the information about alternative populations is based on samples', *Annals of Mathematical Statistics*, 25 (1954), 651–70

ROBERTSON, N. C., BALDWIN, J. A., and HALL, D. J., 'Psychiatric record linkage: a pilot study', University of Aberdeen, Department of Mental Health, Research Report 9, March, 1969

RUSSELL, B., 'On denoting', *Mind*, 14 (1905), 479–93

SMITH, A., 'Preservation of confidence at the central level', in Acheson, E. D. (ed.), *Record linkage in medicine* (Edinburgh and London, 1968), 338–48

STRAWSON, P. F., 'On referring', *Mind*, 9 (1950), 320–44

*SUNTER, A. B., 'A statistical approach to record linkage', in Acheson, E. D. (ed.), *Record linkage in medicine* (Edinburgh and London, 1968), 89–109

TEPPING, B. J., 'Study of matching techniques for subscriptions fulfilment', National Analysts Inc., Philadelphia, August, 1955

TEPPING, B. J., 'A model for optimum linkage of records', *Journal of the American Statistical Association*, 63 (1968), 1321–32

TEPPING, B. J. and CHU, J. T., 'A report on matching rules applied to Reader's Digest data', National Analysts Inc., Philadelphia, August, 1958

WINCHESTER, I., 'The linkage of historical records by man and computer: techniques and problems', *Journal of Interdisciplinary History*, 1 (1970), 107–24

WRIGLEY, E. A. (ed.), *An introduction to English historical demography* (London, 1966)

Glossary

AGGREGATIVE ANALYSIS: used in work on parish registers to denote analysis by simple totals of events, as opposed to techniques like family reconstitution which subdivide populations rather than treating them as an undifferented mass

ALGORITHM: set of operational rules specifying steps by which a problem is to be solved or object to be attained

BINIT WEIGHTS: logarithmic transformations of numbers using logarithms to the base 2

BOOLEAN ARITHMETIC: used in certain types of operations on matrices, notably in establishing reachability; its rules for addition and multiplication are the same as ordinary arithmetic, except that $1 + 1 = 1$

CHAIN: a set of linked records having the property that each record is linked to every other, and that no record is linked to any record outside the chain

CHARACTER STRING: a sequence of digits, symbols or letters of the alphabet

CLUSTER: a set of linked records having the property that every record is linked to at least one other record in the set

COMPARISON SET: a set of records possessing some common characteristic (e.g. all on which the principal is named John Smith) within which a given operation is conducted (e.g. to establish which linked pair of records in the set possesses the strongest link)

FAMILY OF ORIENTATION: family in which an individual is brought up (as opposed to family of procreation which he or she helps to bring into being on marriage)

FAMILY RECONSTITUTION: technique by which records concerning the vital events (birth, marriage and death) of all members of a family are linked to each other

HEURISTIC METHOD: approach to solving a problem which involves successive modifications to course of action in view of the results of earlier steps (i.e. an element of 'learning'), as opposed to a procedure in which action is completely defined before the sequence of operations begins

IDENTIFYING ITEM: an attribute which helps to identify an individual (e.g. occupation, place of residence, age)

INDIVIDUATION: the process of identifying an individual by attributing to him identifying characteristics

INFORMATION FIELD: any class of information which may be present in a record (e.g. name, date, occupation)

INTERGENESIC INTERVAL: period of time between any two successive birth events

LIKELIHOOD RATIOS: a statistic which expresses the relative frequency with which one of two possibilities occurs (e.g. of true and false links in cases where the information fields in pairs of records agree)

LIST PROCESSING: method of data organization by computer which enables a logical structure to be imposed on the data and subsequently modified without altering the physical location of the data

MATCHSCORING: use of a system of giving scores (weights) to links between records (or any other objects in competition with each other) so that the links can be ranked in order of their strength

NODE: used in this book to denote a record or records relating to a single individual and potentially linkable to other records concerning the same individual

REACHABILITY: a term from digraph theory where a point b is said to be reachable from a point a if there is a path from a to b; in this book the concept is used in the discussion of situations where two records are linked only indirectly through one or more intervening records (e.g. a baptism record may be linked to a burial record through an intervening marriage though the baptism and burial are not directly linked, and if so the burial is reachable from the baptism)

RECONSTITUTION: see Family reconstitution

SORTING KEY: an attribute or combination of attributes used to divide a population into subsets (e.g. by surname and forename)

TRANSITIVITY: in digraph theory a digraph is transitive if whenever there is a line ab and a line bc, there is also a line ac; in this book a transitive relation between records is said to exist if when records A and B are linked, and records B and C are linked, A and C are also linkable (transitivity is a defining characteristic of a chain)

Index